To

Time is on your side!

# Money Won't Buy Happiness

BUT TIME TO FIND IT

## Chris Heerlein

REAP Financial
AUSTIN, TEXAS

Chris Heerlein/REAP Financial
9414 Anderson Mill Road
Suite 100
Austin, TX 78729
www.austinsfinancialplanner.com

Book layout ©2013 BookDesignTemplates.com

Money Won't Buy Happiness –But Time to Find It/ Chris Heerlein. — 1st ed.
ISBN 978-1544890432

Photo credits:
Annie Ray, front cover
Tibetan Buddhist Institute, Dalai Lama
Mattias von Corswant, stage shot
Laura Morsman, back cover

# Contents

*To my beautiful wife, Hannah, and my children — Evangeline Ames (age 6), Paloma Jane (Age 4) and Christopher Cash (Age 2) — without whom this book would have been completed 12 months earlier!*

*"An investment in knowledge pays the best interest."*

—BENJAMIN FRANKLIN

# Preface

Baseball legend Yogi Berra is famous for having uttered one-liners that cause your brain to do a double-take. They make no sense at first, but become glowingly profound after you read them three or four times. One of my favorites is: "You can observe a lot by watching."

Working with my mother-in-law, Sandra Newman, a fellow advisor at REAP Financial, I have the privilege of sitting down with hundreds of people each year between the ages of 55 and 70 to discuss their financial futures. Just listening to these folks, whom sociologists have labeled "baby boomers" (born between 1946 and 1964), is an education no money could ever buy. Between Sandra and myself, we've brought in more than $100 million in assets over the last 24 months as of the writing of this book in March 2017, and REAP

Financial has positioned itself as a financial educator to thousands in the Austin, Texas, area. I hope this book will extend that outreach even further.

We discuss portfolios, but that is a sidebar. The real point of our conversations is on a higher plane. It's about how each person can take the money they have saved and invested during their working years and, out of it, forge a comfortable, confident rest of their lives.

It is during this process that I get to know these wonderful people. I am privileged to learn about their lives — their successes, failures, dreams, aspirations and visions for the future. Through it all, I have come to this conclusion: The richest people are not those with mega-mansions and millions in the bank, but those who have a clear vision of what will make them happy and fulfilled.

This is one of the reasons I chose to write this book. I see my job as a financial advisor as sharing what I know about investing and wealth management with people, and helping them find and stay on that happy path. In this book, we will look at the financial landscape from 30,000 feet up — a bird's eye view of concepts and strategies, as opposed to the nuts-and-bolts of financial products and investment management techniques. If you bought this book expecting to find the top 10 stock tips that will make you a Google-illionare in the next six months, or help you outsmart the fat cats on Wall Street, you will probably be disappointed. It's not about getting rich quick, nor is it timing the stock market. The biggest investing lie that has ever been told is, "I know what the market is

> *"Most people agree to co-sign because a bank determined that the other person is not credit-worthy. Guess what? A bank is better at underwriting than you are."*
> *~ John Ulzheimer*

going to do." This book will be about money and investing, so, yes, we will discuss in some detail techniques that can help you accrue, manage, invest, and distribute money. While money won't buy you happiness, there is a direct link between the two things.

While driving down Interstate 35, a highway that bisects Travis County, Texas, where I work and live, I found myself following a motor home with an irritatingly difficult-to-read bumper sticker. I could barely make out the top line: *"Money won't make you happy,"* but I had to get a little too close for comfort to make out the second line, *"But I'd sure as hell like to try!"*

I had to chuckle at just how true that was. I also recognized the quip as coming from a fellow Texan, the late author, speaker and all-around American success story, Zig Ziglar. My all-time favorite Ziglar quote about money is: *"Money isn't the most important thing in life, but it's reasonably close to oxygen on the 'gotta have it' scale."*

"It's time we stop, hey, what's that sound?

Everybody look — what's going down?"

~ Buffalo Springfield

There is change in the air. Based on my research, millennials, the generation born between the late 1980s and the early 2000s, and Gen Xers, born from the early 60s to the late 70s, are better savers than their boomer parents. Problem is, they don't know how or in what to invest. Record numbers of younger individuals these days have seen their friends, parents and co-workers beaten up over the last few years by a volatile stock market. They are hesitant to invest in the market, and are heavy in cash or very low-yielding accounts. With "sleeping" bank rates these days, I venture to say if you're heavy in cash you're losing money safely!

Aggressive investors have little to show for their risk. From 2000 to 2014, the S&P 500 index posted an average annualized return of 4.24 percent for the period ending in 2014. May I repeat,

**4.24 PERCENT!** No matter how you turn it upside down and shake it, that kind of ROI (return on investment) is hardly worth the blood pressure medicine that came with it.[1]

We live in interesting economic times. As host of a financial radio talk show, I am not able to see my audience except through my mind's eye. But when listeners call in with a question and I am able to pass on information that may help them solve a problem or avoid some financial pitfall, it is one of the most gratifying feelings ever.

I have discovered I have a passion for financial education. Some of the most common expressions I hear from the 50-to-70 crowd are "Why didn't I have this conversation years ago?", "Why didn't my CPA tell me I was setting myself up for costly taxes and penalties down the road?" or "If only I had started saving a few years earlier."

> *"Debt keeps you from saving, funding your retirement. … It's almost like you're charging today and mortgaging your future."*
> *~ Cary Carbonaro, CFP*
> *Author of "The Money Queen's Guide"*

Of course there is no way to take all the guesswork out of retirement. The education I provide through my work in radio and television is intended to help eliminate *most* of the guesswork. It is one of the most rewarding privileges I have experienced. Whether it is educating those who are landing their first job today or helping answer the "what next" questions of those who are saying goodbye to the workplace forever, doing what I do is an absolute joy. I hope that comes through in the following pages.

---

[1] Bob Carey. First Trust. Feb. 7, 2017. "A Snapshot of Growth vs. Value Investing." http://www.ftportfolios.com/retail/blogs/marketcommentary/. Accessed Feb. 9, 2017.

Thank you, dear reader, for having come with me this far. If I can be a facilitator in your quest for a richer, more fulfilling life, then it is definitely mission accomplished for me.

# CHAPTER ONE

# Truth About Money

"Don't tell me where your priorities are. Show me where you spend your money, and I'll tell you what they are."
~ James W. Frick

There is a truth about money that does not come from years spent acquiring a formal education or the accumulation of university degrees. It is a truth that can only be found by listening. By sitting down with people of all ages and letting them tell you how money has changed their lives — for good or bad.

The 14th Dalai Lama, the Tibetan monk from whom profundities about Western life flow like a snowmelt in a Rocky Mountain summer, was once asked what surprised him the most about humanity. His answer centered around money:

> "Man, because he sacrifices his health in order to make money. Then he sacrifices his money to recuperate his health. And then he is so anxious about the future that he does not enjoy the present; the result being that he does not live in the present or the future. He lives as if he is never going to die, and then dies having never really lived."

Whether you agree with the Buddhist holy man, his words make you stop and ponder. You may even look up from your work and get one of those thousand-yard stares for a moment before you return to your quest for your weekly paycheck.

All I know about the Dalai Lama is what I have read, but I get the impression he has led a pretty sheltered life. I doubt he has ever struggled to land a job in a recession with a host of other qualified applicants jockeying for a position with résumés in hand. I don't believe he has ever had to wrestle out a weekly paycheck and decide whether he was going to make his car payment or pay his rent.

As Erik Kain pointed out in his *Forbes* article entitled "The Dalai Lama Is Wrong": "Plenty of people do sacrifice their health in one way or another to work and provide. Often, at least in this country, you don't have access to health care unless you work. Many jobs are physically demanding. Even desk jobs can kill you. We can't wish these circumstances away with a clever turn of phrase."[2]

However, that said, the point His Holiness makes is legitimate. In our modern world, it is all too easy to be able to identify the trees and completely get lost in the forest.

---

[2] Erik Kain. Forbes. Oct. 12, 2011. "The Dalai Lama is Wrong." http://www.forbes.com/sites/erikkain/2011/10/12/the-dalai-lama-is-wrong/#57f6c1915e28. Accessed Feb. 9, 2017.

When it comes to clever quotes about the foolishness we Westerners often display over money, I much prefer the wry humor of Will Rogers, that famous American cowboy comedian and satirist of the 1930s, who said, *"Too many people spend money they haven't earned to buy things they don't need to impress people they don't like."*

When you stop and really, really think about what money actually is, it seems silly to contemplate what measures we take to acquire it. In and of itself, money comes down to nothing more than a bunch of numbers. Numbers on a paper bill or on metal discs that jingle in our pockets. Even great monetary wealth is calculated using digits on a computer screen, and those numbers attached to numbers on an account.

So why is money the standard by which many measure themselves and others? The answer is obvious. Because money is more than mere numbers; it has great power to affect our lives, and the lives of those around us.

While it is true that money can't buy happiness, it would be naïve to ignore the power of it, and the many ways it can change our lives.

As one bumper sticker put it: "They say money can't buy happiness. Just give me 100 dollars and watch me smile."

It's the PURPOSE of the money we accumulate not the USE to which it is put that defines whether we are financially successful.

Knowing our "why" when it comes to money will be addressed in this book. I think you will see what I mean.

## The Power of Money

When it comes to quality of life, money can do much to enhance it.

Money may not be able to purchase happiness outright. Miserable misers are almost a proverb. But money can buy us one of the greatest assets of all ... TIME. Time to perhaps find out what we are really searching for.

This truth about money is especially so for young people. In the discussions I have had with many extremely wealthy people — people who are no longer striving but who are able to enjoy all of life's comforts — I find they place a high value on leaving a legacy for their progeny. They want their children and grandchildren to have a life better than theirs, and they want to use their wealth to create this "leg up" on life. They know that, while money can't buy happiness, it can buy education. Education, in turn, can give one time to find the right vocation for him or her self, and thereby enhance that individual's likelihood of achieving happiness in home, career and family.

> "Not everything that can be counted counts, and not everything that counts can be counted."
> ~ Albert Einstein

I have found the most intelligent of these wealthy people are conscious of something else — the potential harm that can come from suddenly possessing large sums of money at a young age, unearned. The question most asked by these individuals is "How can I transfer my wealth to them without ruining their character?" It's a good question.

I think we have all seen this: people falling into large sums of money — whether it's through a windfall, like an inheritance, or something like winning the lottery — their lives coming completely unglued.

Ellen Goodstein, in her piece entitled *"Unlucky in Riches,"* tells the tragic but true tale of several lottery winners and how their lives went from bad to worse:

**Evelyn Adams** won the New Jersey Lottery, not once, but **twice** back to back in 1985 and 1986. Her winnings of $5.4 million dollars are all gone today and Evelyn lives in a trailer.

"Everybody had their hand out," said Evelyn, "and I couldn't say no." She added she also had a gambling habit and lost a big chunk of it at the Atlantic City, New Jersey, casinos.

**William "Bud" Post III** was the lucky winner of the Pennsylvania Lottery to the tune of $16.2 million. His girlfriend broke up with him and then sued him (and won) for a lot of the money. His own brother hired a hitman to kill him in hopes he would inherit a share of the winnings. The plot failed and his brother was arrested, but poor Bud was never the same. Other family members persuaded him to invest in an automobile sales business and restaurant venture in Florida. He never saw any of that money again. Eventually, Bud declared bankruptcy and he now lives on food stamps and $450 per week.

Then there was poor **Willie Hurt** of Lansing, Michigan. In 1989, he won $3.1 million. Two years later, he was a pauper charged with murder. He had squandered his money on a divorce and crack cocaine.

Those are just three of hundreds of sad tales where people became millionaires overnight but failed to address the emotional and psychological aspects of their newfound riches.[3]

According to a 2015 study conducted by CBS Sports, 16 percent of the millionaire players who retire from the National Football League will be broke within 12 years.[4] The study revealed that players with medium-length careers earn an average of $3.2 million in a few years. It's hard for the average Joe who is out there going to the office every day to take home a weekly paycheck to comprehend how these guys could blow such a fortune. But they do.

**Dan Marino,** star quarterback for the Miami Dolphins, excelled on the field, breaking and setting passing records one after another during his NFL career. As an investor, however, he was sacked big time when he sunk millions of dollars into a company called Digital Domain. The company made holograms of dead entertainers performing. I suppose the idea was to produce a "live" concert by musicians who had passed away. In any event, the idea didn't really go over so well, and Marino, who had purchased 1,575,525 shares of the company, lost somewhere in the neighborhood of $14 million.

**Vince Young** is another big-name NFL star who hit bottom after earning a reported $26 million in his six-year stint in pro football with the Tennessee Titans, Philadelphia Eagles and finally the Buffalo Bills. He was reportedly a big spender who also made some bad business decisions along the way.

**Johnny Unitas,** the legendary quarterback whose "golden arm" helped put the then-Baltimore Colts and professional football on the map in the 1950s and 1960s, died in 2002. Players of his era were

---

[3] Ellen Goodstein. Lotto Report. Nov. 8, 2004. "Unlucky in Riches." http://lottoreport.com/AOLSadbuttrue.htm. Accessed Feb. 9, 2017.

[4] Ryan Wilson. CBS Sports. April 15, 2015. "Study: 16 percent of NFL players go bankrupt within 12 years." http://www.cbssports.com/nfl/news/study-16-percent-of-nfl-players-go-bankrupt-within-12-years/. Accessed Feb. 9, 2017.

paid very little by today's standards. His high water mark was $125,000 in 1973. In 1991, Unitas filed for Chapter 11 bankruptcy after he and his partners bought National Circuits Inc., a company that made printed circuit boards for the burgeoning computer industry. The business fell through, and Unitas' dream of becoming part owner of a pro football team in Baltimore went down with it when the bank refused him a loan.

Those are just a few of the sad stories of wealth turning sour and money vanishing in the wind. To relate any more would be depressing. The point is, money has power to change lives, for good and for bad, giving truth to that old adage that goes: "It's not how much you make, it how much you keep that counts."[5, 6]

## Time is Money

We have all heard that time is money. If you are approaching retirement and you think about your youth — when you were in your 20s and 30s — and how much you have learned in the past few decades, you probably say to yourself, "God, if I could just go back and make some of those decisions over."

When we are splashing about in the gurgling, bubbling fountain of youth and the hourglass of our lives is delightfully top-heavy with sand, we carry on as if we are immortal. Most of us soon learn, however, that if we are to be truly financially successful, it is going to require a lifetime of work, responsibility and attention. The sooner we come to that realization, the better.

When you are a teenager, the last thing you think about is retirement. That's altogether understandable. You are breathing

[5] Stacey Bumpus. GoBankingRates.com. Jan. 30, 2015. "How Dan Marino, Vince Young and Other Broke NFL Players Lost Their Fortunes." https://www.gobankingrates.com/personal-finance/dan-marino-vince-young-broke-nfl-players-lost-fortunes/. Accessed Feb. 9, 2017.

[6] Frank Sturm. The Sportster. April 4, 2015. "Top 20 NFL Players Who Lost Everything." http://www.thesportster.com/football/top-20-nfl-players-who-lost-everything/. Accessed Feb. 9, 2017.

that rarified air of what I call "immunity from consequences." Life for you is full of "firsts." First date, first kiss, first car, first job, first mortgage, first baby — Hey! Hold on there, Chris! You're moving a little too fast! Well, that's my point, young reader. Life happens to us, ready or not. What is cool today will be camp in just a few years. While none of us have an expiration date tattooed on our backsides, there is one out there, and you won't last forever.

So, young people, if you are still reading, the sooner you start contemplating your future, the better off you will be. One day, your older self will thank you for it.

We will revisit this later in the book, but there are three phases of money:

- Accumulation
- Preservation
- Distribution

When you're young, you don't worry about the bottom two. But don't miss the accumulation stage, please. You won't enjoy retirement much if you do.

## Lessons in Life

I grew up in Austin, Texas, on the eastern edge of that state's hill country. When I was a mere lad of 14, I would wake up at 4 a.m. every morning, dress hurriedly, scramble outside, find my bicycle, and pedal a mile or so to a small factory warehouse where I casted gold and silver into jewelry until I had to report to school. After school, I pedaled back to work to finish my shift. If you were to blindfold me and put me back there, I would know exactly where I was by the sounds and smells of the place. I remember working with molten metal, pouring the hot, glittery stuff into cast iron molds, and removing it while others worked to finish the pieces. I earned $5 per hour and considered myself lucky to have such a job. Come to think of it, I'm not even sure it would be legal in this day in age to let a 14-year-old kid work in that environment. The owner of the enterprise was a family friend from church. I earned $200 per week! I recall how adult I felt when I was called to the office to receive my first paycheck. But wait just a doggone minute! Something was wrong here!

My paycheck, instead of being made out for $200 was just a little over $150! I wasn't prepared for taxes and the other withdrawals that went along with being on an official payroll.

"What's FICA?" I asked a fellow employee.

"I don't know," the woman replied. "It's just something you have to pay."

It was a lesson in life.

In our family, there wasn't a lot of money to be given. We had to earn it. My father was a Houston police officer who later worked in the commercial security field. My mother was a stay-at-home mom. Money was in short supply most of the time, but love was abundant.

I read somewhere that it was George Bernard Shaw who came up with the phrase, "youth is wasted on the young." I don't much agree with ol' George. He must have been a cynical old curmudgeon who was jealous of young people and their free-spiritedness and carefree existence. One thing I do believe, however, is that youth is a tremendous gift. It affords its recipients golden opportunities that many youths today find ways to squander.

There is an old French saying that, when translated, goes like this: "If only youth had the knowledge; if only old age had the strength." The truth of that starts to sink in after three or four decades of life. It's somewhere in those middle years that you realize you can no longer leap tall buildings in a single bound, and that your Kryptonite is your bad cholesterol count. I consider myself very fortunate to have had the opportunity to learn the value of money (and the value of saving it) the hard way. The hard way is not necessarily the best way, however.

## Basic Money Education

Was personal finance part of the curriculum at your high school? It wasn't at mine. In my informal research I still don't see much emphasis placed on it. Why is that? Shouldn't preparing our children for the real world include basic education in personal finance? I wonder how many of our young people understand the difference between simple and compound interest. How many know the elemental things about Wall Street and the stock markets of the world? I wonder how many know how to balance a checkbook or read a bank statement?

When public schools teach teenagers how to drive a car, they warn them of the dangers of the road. But where do they learn about the dangers of credit card debt? How many of them enter adult life and fail financially because of this lack of education? Do the lesson planners think personal finance is over their heads? If so, they are mistaken.

*"Courage is being scared to death but saddling up anyway."*

*~ John Wayne*

You don't even have to be good at math to understand the essential concepts of earning, saving and investing. How many lives would be positively impacted by carving out just a few hours of teaching time to let them understand the power of setting aside 10 percent of their income for the future?

## The Miracle of Compound Interest

What follows may seem like basic stuff — and it is! But from my conversations with young people, it is evident that so few have a clue about such matters. So, I felt compelled to put a paragraph or two about the "miracle" of compound interest in this book. If you already know this, please pass it on to the future leaders of the nation!

Albert Einstein reportedly called compound interest the eighth wonder of the world. I suppose he was amazed at how it can transform a small amount of money into a huge amount of money *over time*. Time is the key ingredient. The more time you have, the bigger the transformation.

Here's the way it works: when you invest or save money, it earns interest. Let's say you place a sum of money into an account. The next year, assuming you don't touch it, you earn interest on the original sum, *plus* interest on the interest. In the third year, you earn interest on the original sum, *plus* interest on the first two years, and so forth and so on. Earning interest on interest and then earning more interest on that interest can be likened to a snowball rolling downhill. It starts slow and small but builds upon itself. It increases in momentum and size until, depending on how far it rolls, it's as big as a house! If you started at the top of the hill, your snowball, by the time it reached the bottom of the hill, would be much bigger than someone's snowball if they started, let's say, in the middle of the hill.

The earlier you start saving and investing, the more money you have at the end of the trail. Here's an example:

You probably learned the story of Christopher Columbus in elementary school — how in 1492 he "sailed the ocean blue" to discover the New World. Well, let's imagine Columbus found a penny on his way to visit Queen Isabella. And let's say, rather than putting that penny in his pocket, or spending it, he put the coin in an account earning 6 percent interest.

Now, let's say ol' Chris picked one of his friends and told them to leave the penny there, but remove the interest every year, and put that interest in a piggy bank. The total value collected in that piggy bank would eventually accumulate to a bit more than 30 cents today. No big shakes, right? But here's where it gets interesting. If

Columbus had placed that penny in an account returning 6 percent interest, and just allowed the interest to compound for all these centuries, guess how much the account would be worth today? Over $121 billion dollars!

If you don't believe me, I discovered this little illustration in 2009, which is 517 years from 1492. To check this out, just get out your calculator, and multiply $.01 times 1.06 percent, and hit the enter key 517 times. If you don't get carpal tunnel syndrome first, you should come up with $121,096,709,346.21.

> *"I am a great believer in luck, and I find the harder I work, the more I have of it."*
> *~ Thomas Jefferson*

Can you see now why Albert Einstein was so impressed with compound interest? Okay, okay. So, you are not going to live 517 years to collect billions on your one-cent investment, but it makes the point that saving small amounts when you're young can enable you to have a substantial amount of money later on.

For a more practical example, consider the case of Betty, age 22, who starts working after college, and can save $300 per month in an account earning 6 percent compound interest. By age 28, she decides to quit working and raise a family. She stops contributing the $300 per month; she just leaves the money in the account and lets it grow. If Betty never contributed *another cent* to her account, by the time she turned 65 she would have about $230,000, despite contributing less than $27,000.

Remember the snowball that started rolling downhill in the middle of the hill? That represents people who get started late. But to show you how powerful compound interest can be, let's say Ted started saving at the same pace as Betty when he turned 39. While Betty stopped working and saving and just let her interest grow,

Ted must continue contributing his $300 per month for more than 26 years without interruption to retire with the same amount. The total amount contributed by Ted over that period will be $93,600. Why the big difference? Because Betty's money had more *time* to grow at compound interest.

## The Other Side of the Coin

The thing about interest is it works both ways. You pay interest when you borrow, just as you earn interest when you save or invest.

Compound interest can be an ugly curse when it's on the debit side of the ledger. Revolving-charge accounts can kill you with interest charges of 25 percent or more. When you are young, debt sneaks up on you and you can get into trouble before you know what hit you. Here's a little history lesson on this phenomenon:

## The Birth of the Credit Card

Store credit has been around for ages. It started back in colonial days when America was more agricultural than industrial. Farmers whose payday came once a year would run up a tab at the local general store. When they harvested and sold their crops, they would pay off the debt.

Years later, in the early 1900s, the idea spread to cities when large department stores began to extend credit to customers with "most favored buyer" status. Still later, it became customary for these stores to issue proprietary "charge plates," good in just that one store only.

Following World War II, America experienced an economic boom. There was great demand for everything. The "buy now, pay later" idea soon took the nation by storm. Charge accounts became more popular. "Will that be cash or charge?" was the tempting offer put forth at the end of every sales transaction in department stores across the country in the 1950s.

In fact, according to the people at MasterCard, the "Charge-It" card was the first bank card, introduced in 1946 by John Biggins, a banker in Brooklyn, New York. When you bought something with your Charge-It card, the bill went to Biggins' bank, where the charges were deducted from your account there. That was the big catch. You had to have an account at Biggins' bank.

In 1950, Diners Club credit cards were born. In those days, it was a real club for people who wanted to eat now and pay later. Within just a few years, the card was in widespread use and could be used to buy merchandise. After Diners Club came Master Charge (now MasterCard) and Bank Americard (now Visa). All the others followed. [7]

The first credit cards were paper, not plastic. The reason for the plastic cards was so account numbers could be embossed as a method of preventing fraud. The raised letters were stamped there to discourage fraud and make checkout easier. In the old days, clerks used knuckle-busters, a device that rolled across the raised numbers to imprint them on cards and give the card owner a carbon paper (Carbon paper? What's that?) receipt. Those machines are virtually gone now, having been replaced by electronic devices that read magnetic strips, or, for the latest in credit card security tech, small microchips.

## The Blessing Becomes a Curse

What began as a great convenience to consumers has led to more financial ruin and heartache than anyone could have imagined during those early days of buy now, pay later. For those who couldn't control their spending, easy credit was like heroin to a junkie. It quickly got out of control. CreditCards.com estimates

---

[7] Ben Woolsey and Emily Starbuck Gerson. Credit Cards.com. June 15, 2016. "The history of credit cards." http://www.creditcards.com/credit-card-news/credit-cards-history-1264.php. Accessed Feb. 9, 2017.

about 167 million American adults own at least one credit card, and the average American household debt is $5,750. Those averages don't tell the whole story, though. Those statistics figure in all those who pay their card balances off as soon as they receive their bill, as well as those who carry large balances, and "borrow from Peter to pay Paul" just to keep out of bankruptcy. Of those who carry balances, the average debt is a crushing $15,799.[8, 9]

Many young consumers fall into the "minimum payment due" trap and dig themselves deeper and deeper into the hole.

This is one reason why, when I sit down with young clients to plan for their financial futures, the first thing we work on is getting to a point of financial health first. Translation: forging a plan to pay off burdensome credit card debt.

## The Minimum Payment Trap

If you want to make the credit card companies love you, just pay them the minimum payment due each month. Why? Because you will likely never pay off the balance, which means you will be paying interest to the credit card company forever. Let's do a little math: The minimum payment is usually 2-4 percent of the total due. So let's say you have a credit card balance of $5,000. Let's say the credit card company is extremely generous to you and gives you a 2 percent minimum payment. Fantastic! All you have to pay them is $100 and you can forget about it until next month, right? Let's say you don't charge anything else to the card and you pay your minimum payment on time. Your balance would go down by the payment amount, less the interest charges for that month.

[8] Jamie Golzalez-Garcia. CreditCards.com. Oct. 25, 2016. "Credit card ownership statistics." http://www.creditcards.com/credit-card-news/ownership-statistics.php. Accessed Feb. 9, 2017.

[9] Robert Harrow. ValuePenguin.Nov. 28, 2016. "Average Credit Card Debt in America: 2016 Facts & Figures." https://www.valuepenguin.com/average-credit-card-debt. Accessed Feb. 9, 2017.

So where's the trap?

Here's the trap: The next month, when you get your statement you will see that minimum payment is a little lower. If you just pay that minimum payment, you are doing two things (1) prolonging the period of time the company can charge you interest, and (2) tempting yourself to use it again. My advice, dear young reader, is to pay it off and cut it up as soon as possible. Failing that, pick an amount you can afford and pay that amount every month, regardless of what the minimum payment is, and **then** get out the scissors and cut it up. You will be happy you did. If you are the American with seven credit cards carrying a total balance of more than $15,000 annually, let me suggest you isolate which cards charge the most interest and pay those off first. After you pay off the last dollar, have a card-cutting ceremony. In fact, if you are of legal drinking age, toast yourself with a glass of champagne. Just make sure you buy the champagne with cash!

There is a reason why you often hear expressions like "in over your head" and "under water" used for being in debt. When you are in debt, you can't breathe. There is no sweeter air than that lungful you gulp when you come out of the water after having held your breath for a minute or so. It's almost as good as the debt-free feeling you get when you pay off your last charge card. The only way to make compound interest work *for* you is to be in a position where it is not working **against** you.

## Easy to Say; Hard to Do

I am going to say this, knowing how difficult it is to do, especially when you are young. There is no good reason to have any debt for anything with the possible exception of a mortgage on your home. If I'm your advisor, I am going to encourage you to pay cash for everything, even your cars. Remember the penny Christopher

Columbus found? Every little spoonful you can cram into a savings account now will come back to you in buckets when you retire. To help you accomplish that, please consider some of the following saver skill sets. The more of them you master, the more wealth you can accumulate for your eventual retirement.

> *"Someone's sitting in the shade today because someone planted a tree a long time ago."*
> ~ *Warren Buffett*

**Live within your means.** First, you must understand your means. How much money do you earn? What are your necessary expenses, such as food, clothing, shelter and transportation? Put them on paper. You have just created a budget and that's where this skill begins. The rest is just discipline. Once your budget is established, your challenge is to find places where you can either spend less or earn more to achieve your financial goals.

Do you *need* a new car? Or do you just *want* a new car? A lesson I learned early in life while making $5 per hour smelting jewelry was this: You can either have the something you want to buy with the money you earn, or you can have the money itself. But you can't have both. Once you spend a dollar, that dollar is gone, gone, gone. And so is the power of that dollar to replicate itself through compound interest. If you pluck whatever you want from the store shelves and put it on credit, ask yourself if you really want to pay compound interest on a pair of sneakers, or a pair of designer jeans?

When you are salivating for it, it is easy to trick yourself into rationalizing that a luxury is actually a need.

"Hey, designer jeans are clothing, and clothing is a need," you may tell yourself. All the while, we know the truth, don't we?

**Take charge of your own financial future.** People seem eager to advise other people on just about anything, whether they know anything about the subject or not. Nothing elicits human good nature more than someone who is lost and needs directions. If you don't believe this, just stop your car, lower your window and ask someone where the nearest interstate is. No matter what their disposition is under ordinary circumstances, they will usually try to help you. Even if they haven't a clue where the interstate is, they still want to help you get there.

You will also get advice from well-meaning souls about managing your finances, even when they know very little about the subject. It could be your neighbor who knows somebody who has a cousin in Chicago who gave him a tip on a stock that can't lose. It could be your Aunt Mildred, who really wants you to buy a house, even though you can only afford one of those treacherous adjustable-rate mortgages. It is crucial that you take charge of managing your financial future, or someone else will attempt to manage — or mismanage — it for you.

Even some unscrupulous people who call themselves financial professionals will give you a bum steer. Ever heard of Bernie Madoff? Then there are those well-meaning folks who can run your financial ship aground. They mean well, they just don't know what they are doing. The point is, *you* must take charge of your *own* financial future. Read books on personal finance. Know how much you are spending, saving and earning. Know where you have your savings and why you have it there. Ask questions of your banker, or whoever represents the custodian in whose hands you have placed your "rainy day money." If you get financial statements, open them, read them and, if you don't understand them, ask questions until you do. I can't encourage you enough to get to the bottom of any fees you are paying in your accounts. Let me ask you this question: How do you hold your advisor, broker or money manager accountable to performance if you don't even know what you're paying them? ... Exactly!

**Save it now and spend it later.** I saw a clever cartoon the other day. Two neighbors were talking over a fence. The mailbox told you that the neighbor who was speaking was named Jones. Jones says to his neighbor, "I'm sorry to hear that you were keeping up with us ... we just declared bankruptcy." Don't let yourself become unduly influenced by your friends to overspend. Just because your friend is driving a new Lexus shouldn't move you to buy one, too, if you can't afford it. If your friends fly to the Greek islands for a scenic cruise and you can't afford to go along, say no graciously but firmly. Remember your savings goals and stay faithful to your plan. If you want to pay off your credit card more than you want to go clubbing, don't go clubbing just because your friends are doing it. Let your friends in on why you are turning down their invitations so they'll know that you're rejecting the expense and not their company.

**Pinch pennies; they make dollars later on.** Within reason, cut costs whenever possible. Buy things when they're on sale. Clip coupons. Eat before you go to the movies instead of "investing" in popcorn, candy and drinks. Come to think about it, wait until the movie comes out on DVD and rent it from the dollar vending machine around the corner! Eat before you go to a restaurant and then order an

> "Successful investing takes time, discipline and patience. No matter how great the talent or effort, some things just take time."
> ~ Warren Buffett

appetizer. Have fun, but make a supreme effort to stick to your budget and your savings plan without being too weird. Keep thinking of that penny Columbus found.

**Stay on budget during the holidays.** This is a tough one, especially if you are the kind to easily get caught up in the joy of the Christmas season. If you are the gregarious sort and you love giving gifts, plan well ahead when *"Jingle Bells"* isn't ring-ting-tingling and you aren't humming carols. That way you will be able to accommodate your holiday spirit without becoming a total Grinch. Guard the carefree retirement you are saving for *and* avoid all the lines.

**Develop good spending/saving habits.** If you want to create a new habit, whether it's eating a piece of fruit for lunch, getting more exercise, or posting your blog every day, behavior experts say it takes 21 days to form a new habit. Once you are in a habit of consulting your budget before spending money frivolously, you will do it automatically, even if you do the math in your head. It's the same with savings. Chunk that money into your savings account every paycheck until it becomes your financial heartbeat. Years from now, somewhere on a sandy beach, your older self will find your younger self and sincerely thank you.

Discipline and Structure = Success

As you can probably tell by now, the true purpose and passion behind this book is helping not only those who are knocking on the door of retirement in the next five to 10 years, but also helping young people find the discipline and structure they need to forge a comfortable financial future.

When you are in or approaching retirement, your monetary wealth may be among your greatest assets. When you are young, and have not yet accumulated your fortune, your greatest assets are your *TIME* and your *POTENTIAL*.

I don't think you can put too great a value on that. If you want to start saving and investing, let's talk about it. Not too many of you are going to have a large lump sum of money fall into your lap. Not many young people are in line for five-figure bonuses or six-figure incomes just yet. If you are in ladder-climbing mode, you are trying to accumulate all the things that compose the American Dream, and most of them are tangibles right now, such as granite countertops, the new car and all the other stuff you feel you must have. I get that. We need to put money into our living and our lifestyle. But if you are making $1,100 per week, just scrape the $100 off the top and put it into savings. Or invest it where you can have meaningful growth. If you can save 10-15 percent per year in your 20s — and even early 30s — you are on a path to be able to maintain your standard of living down the road in retirement. Scraping those dollars off the top now, and doing it automatically, can allow you to amass a sizable amount of money in a relatively short period — quicker than you can imagine.

# CHAPTER TWO

# The Phantom Millionaire

"They say there are two sides to every story, and three when the truth gets told."

~ Drake

E very week, I get to meet people from both ends of the financial spectrum; from those who have little to no savings to those who have millions stashed away in banks, CDs, brokerage accounts and investments. What amazes me is that people who have many millions of dollars don't necessarily act any differently than those who live from paycheck to paycheck.

One wealthy client, for whom we handle millions of dollars, was scheduled to come in for his annual review. About 45 minutes before his appointment, he called the office to say he was sorry, but he was going to miss his appointment because his car was broken down on the side of the road.

"Can we help you in some way?" our sweet receptionist offered.

"No, it's just this old car of mine," he said. "The tow-truck is on its way."

We're talking about a man who has millions of dollars and no debt. This is someone who could certainly pay cash for a new car. Instead, he chooses to drive a 12-year-old Chevrolet.

It's that way with most of our super-wealthy clients. Few of them drive automobiles that show off their status. More of them pull up in 10-year-old Camrys and Hondas than do in a brand new black Mercedes. This teaches us something about human nature and the principles of financial success, doesn't it? Perhaps the reason they are so well off is they have shunned flashier, unnecessary things all their lives and have saved and invested the money it would have taken to buy them. They are secure with themselves. Comfortable in their own skin, as they say. They have no need to show off for others, because they have the quiet calm of knowing their worth.

On the other side of that coin are those who may be struggling financially, but from the lifestyle they live you would never know it. They go deep in debt trying to put on the appearance of wealth — which is why real wealth eludes them.

## What It Takes to Be a Millionaire

There are some instant millionaires out there, I'm sure, but for the most part, it is a rare thing for someone under the age of 50 to have saved anywhere near $1 million. Those who attain that financial success mark usually do so because they are highly organized, educated and intelligent people who set financial goals and stick with them. By education I am not necessarily talking about formal education. The woods are full of individuals with many years of university training, but who are not financially successful. On the other hand, those with an entrepreneurial spirit who will let nothing stand in the way of achieving their goals make up the vast majority of self-made millionaires.

I have also found that in nine out of 10 cases, these individuals are hard-core savers. It is almost like a religion to them. They wake up each day, sip their coffee and sniff the air, and decide how they can earn and save more than they did the day before.

They are not wasteful, either.

Sandra Newman, my mother-in-law, is a good example of such thrifty behavior. I have known my wife's mother since I was 13 years old, and at some point, I noticed she reuses Ziploc bags three and four times. Although she could well afford to toss the old baggie in the trash and use a new one, she takes the time to wash out the old one, careful not to tear the plastic, and puts leftover meals in them.

"Why do you do that?" I asked.

"Do what?" she said.

"Reuse the plastic baggies," I said.

"Because, Chris," she began scornfully. "It's wasteful to throw perfectly good things into the garbage."

Can't argue with that, now, can you?

She has a thing about tinfoil, too. If there's not too much stuck to it, she happily folds it up and tucks it in a drawer for reuse. This amazing woman, who has taught me and so many others such valuable lessons about what it means to scrimp and save for an end goal, practices what she preaches. She believes — and it is true — that when saving and thriftiness are habits, financial success will follow.

Self-made millionaires are not afraid of risk, but it must be calculated risk. They do not just throw money at the stock market, blindly trusting it will produce returns.

In my line of work, I hear all the horror stories of fortunes lost by individuals who allowed their sentiment to get in the way of good judgment, and of individuals who made financial decisions without all the facts. Some were flippant, kneejerk investments their sons or daughters talked them into that didn't pan out. I have known some who jeopardized their own retirement by taking an uncalculated risk for a son or daughter. The instinct to protect one's children is strong, and it can override good, common sense. Some, because of this sentimental chink in their armor, may have to someday move in with those same children.

The self-made millionaires I have met are not stingy. Instead they calculate before they spend. Most of them live comfortable, but not lavish, lives. For most of them, life is best enjoyed if it is stable.

## Most Will Never Be Millionaires

As much as I hate to say it, most people out there are never going to be able to acquire seven figures going into retirement. Statistics bear this out. It just is what it is.

Each year, the U.S. Census Bureau publishes statistics on how many millionaires there are in the United States. Going by net worth, in 2015, there were approximately 10.1 million people with $1 million or more. Even as a record number of people hit the "illionaire" mark, it's only about 3 percent of the population.[10]

By the way, if anyone doubts that America is the land of opportunity, consider the fact that the U.S. has more **HNWIs** (High Net Worth Individuals, $1 million or more) than any other country in the world, hands down. I will pass along some more statistics on wealth building later in this book, but suffice it to say that most people just don't have enough money heading into retirement. If you are reading this book, chances are you either aren't or won't be among the underprepared. Especially if you can focus on a strategy of slow and sustained saving, and growing your investments at a steady pace. That simple approach will positively affect your life and promote your security in retirement, whatever your numbers amount to when you are ready to pull the trigger.

---

[10] Robert Frank. CNBC. March 7, 2016. "Record number of millionaires living in the US." http://www.cnbc.com/2016/03/07/record-number-of-millionaires-living-in-the-us.html. Accessed Feb. 9, 2017.

## Saving How Much?

"I am just now starting to save for my retirement. How much of my paycheck should I save?" That was a question asked of me recently on our weekly *"Retire Ready"* radio program. It is a frequently asked question and I always give the same answer because it is a formula based on age.

Obviously, the longer you wait (remember the snowball rolling downhill in Chapter One), the more you need to save to maintain your current lifestyle when you retire. When listeners hear it, some are surprised, others are not. Some are already saving that much and more. Others save very little. Here's a handy guideline for milestones to shoot for:

- At age 35, have a years' worth of your current salary saved.
- At age 45, have three years' salary saved.
- At age 55, have five years' salary saved.
- At age 67 (retirement), have eight to 11 times your current annual salary saved.

If you are in your middle years, before you swallow your tongue, those savings can include such things as an employer match on your 401(k) and tax refunds.

As Ben Franklin so famously said, "A penny saved is a penny earned." One way to make the savings burden bearable as you are preparing for your eventual retirement is to pare down your lifestyle in areas of extravagance. Separate needs from wants, and live not **within** your means but **below** your means until you catch up. Another Zig Ziglar quote I am fond of is: *"By the mile, it's a trial; by the inch, it's a cinch."* Translation: when you are formulating your budget, take your budget cuts in small steps. For instance, $100 per month. You would be surprised at how quickly cutting out some unnecessary expenses can quickly add up to $100 per month. Skip two restaurant dinners and eat at home each month, and you are there. Forego a few lunches each month and that will do it too. You can slowly start working into a new pattern of life that will make little difference in lifestyle points, but will quickly add up on the savings end of things.

You know yourself far better than anyone else ever will. What can you think of that you can skip, omit, cast off, do without or otherwise cut out of your expenditures and (very important) slide that over to the savings column? Probably quite a few things, if you are honest with yourself.

Successful retirement has changed from our grandparents' day. Being able to retire comfortably in America in this era is being able to wake up in the morning without the burden of debt and be content with the things you have. It will require discipline to achieve that end, true, but those who have done so will tell you it is worth it in the long run. When I talk on the radio about the "changing story of retirement," I spend most of my time talking about reality checks. Separating what you think you can do from what you can actually do, financially.

*"It takes as much energy to wish as to plan."*

*~ Eleanor Roosevelt*

My wife, Hannah, calls me a workaholic sometimes.

Another old saying comes to mind: "Choose a job you love, and you will never have to work a day in your life." It may appear that I take families through the same process each time, but it is not at all repetitive. Why? Because every situation is different. Every person is different. Everyone has different goals, aspirations, dreams and separate visions for their retirements.

"I have one of the best jobs in the world, you know," I told Hannah. "I have the opportunity each day to improve a client's 'return on life'."

I like to think of my role as helping clients with their return on life, or ROL, as opposed to the traditional approach of trying to improve the client's portfolio ROI — return on investment.

In some cases, people come into my office thinking their dreams are unachievable — too far away from them, financially and chronologically, to be attainable. It is exciting for me to be able to coach them and guide them to the point where they can see that dream take on shape and probability.

No two people are alike physically, emotionally, psychologically, and certainly not financially. Even identical twins, who have the same DNA, have different fingerprints. Consider this: two people may work at the same office or factory, be the same age, have the same size family, earn the same income, own identical houses, and share identical portfolios, but it would be virtually impossible for them to have identical financial plans. Why is that? Because it would be highly improbable they would share the same goals in life. It's not the dollar amount that's at the center of a financial plan; it's what you want to **do** with the money.

Out of the thousands of portfolios we have analyzed, we have never encountered a situation where, when we isolated the *purpose* of the portfolio, we found it to be the same as another.

# CHAPTER THREE

# Spend Money to Save Money

"It's tax time. I know this because I'm staring at documents that make no sense to me, no matter how many beers I drink."
~ Dave Berry

R un that by me again. Did you say *spend* money to *save* money?

I can see the wheels of your mind spinning that phrase around, trying to make sense of it. I will admit that it is a novel and unconventional approach, but bear with me and you will see what I mean, dear reader.

As an investment and retirement advisor, income planning coach, whatever you wish to call me, I see people in my profession usually talking about pinching pennies and squeezing nickels until the buffalo bellows. We advisors are usually on TV, radio, or even in client meetings, advocating, "Save, save, save." And it is true that saving is the cornerstone of successful retirement planning. Rarely will I ever tell people to spend money frivolously, but there are a few rare cases. Let me explain.

Once we set about creating a retirement plan for a family and we have put together a coordinated income plan for them — one that helps ensure they are not going to run out of money in their golden years — then we have created a spending zone for them. The spending zone is an amount that they may spend with confidence. If that is your situation, and you have been saving for that vacation in the Caribbean, and there is no other pressing need for your cash, then by all means, *GO!* and don't worry that you will be spending money you will need down the road to pay bills and meet expenses. That's in the bag. It's taken care of.

> *"Wealth is not his that has it,*
> *but his that enjoys it."*
> *~ Benjamin Franklin*

The "save, save, save" message is meant for people in what we call the accumulation years of their lives. These are people in their 20s, 30s, 40s, or, if they got started late, even their 50s, people who have yet to lock in their lifetime incomes. Each financial situation is different, of course, but many Americans spend far too much in the accumulation years, and regret it when suddenly retirement is staring them in the face.

When we are in our working years, we may be used to seeing our retirement accounts growing. We expect them to go up every year. It all depends on how the stock market is performing, of course. But then, when we retire, instead of putting money into those accounts, we find ourselves in a position where we must take money out of them. It is then that an interesting psychological phenomenon occurs. When we see that number on the bottom of the page shrinking instead of expanding, we suddenly become more frugal. We don't spring for the check so easily when dining out with friends. We drive around looking for the lowest price at the gasoline pumps. We count our change studiously and ask for the senior citizen's discount without hesitation or embarrassment.

Why? The reasons are simple — (a) we don't know how long we are going to live, and (b) we are dealing with finite, nonrenewable resources.

One couple with whom I was conducting a first-interview survey of their economic situation told me they loved to travel. Part of my job is to determine what clients want out of life. I must know that before I can help them get it.

"We love to travel," the woman said. "But we are afraid to go anywhere right now. We always thought that when we retired we would be able to take a tour of the Holy Land and see some of the places mentioned in the Bible. But we are putting that on the back burner."

"Why do you feel that way?" I asked.

"Because we would have to pull at least $4,000 out of our retirement savings account, and we just think it would be irresponsible to do that," the man replied.

I didn't argue with them. It was a perfectly understandable sentiment **IF** they did not have a guaranteed income in place that would ensure they wouldn't run out of resources down the road. I am happy to report, within a year of that interview, these nice folks could take their dream vacation and see the Holy Land, and even take a European river cruise. What made this happen? They arranged their accounts so a portion of their retirement income was fixed for life. This left them with enough discretionary funds to travel without fear of tapping into money they would need for everyday expenses.

Where I live and work in Austin, the weather is unpredictable. We have floods, we have droughts. It's hot one day, and cold the next. Occasionally, it will even snow (not much, maybe an inch or two every year or so). As one old timer says about Austin's weather: "The weather here is great. Just don't get attached to it because it is bound to change."

When it rains, the Colorado River, which bisects Austin, is prone to flooding, and the dams on the river do their best to keep these floods under control. Sometimes these large flood-control dams are overwhelmed, as they were in the spring of 2016. But they usually do their jobs reasonably well. In dry times, the water level in the lakes behind the dams on the Colorado drops. The man-made lakes fill up again when the rainy spells come. But the idea of the dam system is to keep the river flow constant. It's that way with spending. It needs to be controlled to offset the constantly changing conditions of the economy, the vagaries of the market and the unpredictability of individual needs. That is why I meet with my clients every six months if not more. The economy can change very quickly, and without notice. But your expenses will likely remain constant throughout retirement. The more confident you are that you are in no danger of running out of money, the freer you will be to spend your money on the things you need, thus maintaining or enhancing your quality of life.

I do not like to see my clients scrimping, having to drive around in cars that are past their prime, or having to re-sole their tennis shoes six times before they buy new ones. Not if I can help it. That's no way to live. Sometimes — and I will repeat this once more — you must *spend* money to *save* money. What does that mean exactly? For example, it's often easier to go ahead and spend the money it takes to buy a decent, quality automobile — one that will last and not cost you so much in repair bills — than it is to buy an El Cheapo rust bucket that will fall apart on you. The same goes for clothing, appliances, furniture.

Penny-pinching out of fear can be costlier in the long run, forcing you to buy inferior quality products or sacrifice protecting your valuable assets. It doesn't have to be that way if you will do just a little planning.

## Will You Ever Have Enough?

How much money do I need to have acquired in my savings before I can safely and comfortably retire? That's a great question. And the answer is, "it depends." That is why you should sit down with a financial advisor — a fiduciary with your best interests (and not commissions) at heart, and figure out that number. The key in determining the "right number" for you is to first ascertain how long your income will last. To do that, you must have a general idea of what your spending will be. Calculate what your expenses are now and what they will be once you have pulled the plug on your paycheck and have

*"It's good to have money and the things that money can buy, but it's good, too, to check up once in a while and make sure that you haven't lost the things that money can't buy."*

*~ George Lorimer*

started living off your stored assets. That's how you can know whether you will be able to retire sooner rather than later.

I meet with a lot of people in my office who think they are **years** out from retirement. Sometimes **years** and **years!** I often end up showing them how they can retire sooner than they had imagined. Naturally, I like those kinds of meetings. They have happy endings. It's an awesome feeling for the clients, and for me, because I could add to the quality of their lives.

But some labor under delusions that have been created by myths and old wives' tales propagated years ago by financial professionals, either out of ignorance or out of greed. A case in point would be the 4-5 percent withdrawal theory, sometimes called the 4 Percent Withdrawal Rule. For years, some financial professionals have told their clients, if they can keep their withdrawals between 4 and 5 percent of their portfolio's assets, they will be able to live a comfortable retirement and not run out of money. The idea behind this theory is that you should earn at least 4-5 percent on your money, so the wheel of the financial-perpetual-motion machine should keep turning. Sounds good, right? But let's look at what the markets have provided us in the past decade.

The first decade of the 21$^{st}$ century has been dubbed the "lost decade" by some in the financial industry because returns went up and down, but essentially didn't go anywhere. When examined over the long haul, stock market returns during that period barely kept up with paltry returns of savings accounts and bank CDs.

In the economic environment that prevails as of the writing of this book in March 2017, I cannot conscientiously advise a retired investor to withdraw anywhere near 4-5 percent of a market based portfolio and promise them they would not run out of money.

## Maybe vs. Certain

Here's something to think about. If an income plan is based *solely* on the performance of the stock market, regardless of how smart or savvy your investment advisor or mutual fund manager or stock broker may be, it is a "maybe" income plan. Anyone who tells you differently is blowing smoke. The theory of the 4 Percent Withdrawal Rule became popular in the 1990s when the stock market was on a roll. According to this rule, retired investors could safely withdraw 4 percent from their brokerage accounts each year for 30 years and never run out of money. It was developed by William P. Bengen, a financial planner in California, who plugged in several combinations of numbers: (a) rates of withdrawal, (b) allocation of assets, and (c) duration of retirement. He then came up with the magic number — 4.5 percent. He got there by using decades of historical data available at the time. Bengen maintained that, provided a portfolio was balanced with 60 percent stocks and 40 percent bonds and adjusted periodically, it could produce income for 30 years, even withstanding inflation of 4 percent, before the investor ran out of money.

Just to make the math easy, suppose you had $1 million parked with a brokerage house. Under Bengen's assumption, you could live on a $40,000 withdrawal per year, adding slightly to it each year for inflation. You could then live on that for 30 years, or until the end of your life, whichever came first, and not run out of money. Stockbrokers adopted the theory as the Holy Grail of market-based income planning for retirement. Most of them have now seen the light, but I still come across many who are still pounding that square peg into its round hole.

Bengen was no dummy. He graduated from the Massachusetts Institute of Technology before becoming a financial planner, and successfully managed a soft-drink bottling company. So what was the problem? He was basing his theory on incomplete data. He didn't figure in the stock market reversals of 2000 and 2008. Why? Because they hadn't happened yet.

An article entitled "Say Goodbye to the 4% Rule" written by Kelly Greene in the March 1, 2013, issue of the Wall Street Journal said the following:

"If you had retired Jan. 1, 2000, with an initial 4% withdrawal rate and a portfolio of 55% stocks and 45% bonds rebalanced each month, with the first year's withdrawal amount increased by 3% a year for inflation, your portfolio would have fallen by a third through 2010, according to investment firm T. Rowe Price Group. And you would be left with only a 29% chance of making it through three decades, the firm estimates."

So, what was "virtually guaranteed" turned out not to be guaranteed at all. It was a "maybe" income plan.

"Forget the 4% Withdrawal Rule" was an article published by *Money* magazine in 2014. It quoted Wade Pfau, professor of retirement income at The American College, who lowered the 4 percent withdrawal projection down to *2.22 percent!* So, assuming you started with $1 million in your portfolio, that's living on a little over $20,000 per year. Not many people I interview could successfully live on that amount.

I think it is safe to say the so-called 4 Percent Withdrawal Rule is officially dead, but some financial advisors out there have just not gotten the memo.

## Projections vs. Guarantees

I have a music background. I love the sound of a well-made acoustic guitar. The 1962 J-45 Gibson is the favorite of my collection. These fine instruments can produce beautiful music. But not if the strings are out of tune. Nothing grates on my ears more than an out-of-tune guitar. All it takes is one string on a six-string guitar to be a half-note off pitch to ruin an otherwise beautiful song.

> *"There is a gigantic difference between earning a great deal of money and being rich."*
> *~ Marlene Dietrich*

To me, an income plan that does not harmonize with your goals, lifestyle and purpose is like that out-of-tune guitar. If you are interested in having a guaranteed income that will last you for the rest of your life, and you start hearing words like: "projection," "estimated," "approximately" and "probably" when you are discussing it with your advisor, then it is a "maybe" income plan. That is perfectly okay if that's what you want. But if you are looking for lifetime income plans, listen for the key words that harmonize with that thought. Income should be absolute, not maybe!

## A Good Time to Catch Up

Maybe it's that time of life. You just turned 50. The kids are grown and gone. You turn to your significant other and you say,

"Honey, we have 15 more years before retirement. We have got to start saving for this!"

Well, Uncle Sam heard you and has made it easier for you to do that very thing. The government calls them "catch-up contributions." At the end of the year, individuals who are age 50 or over can make annual catch-up contributions to the tune of thousands of dollars to individual retirement accounts, 401(k)s, 403(b)s, SEPs (simplified employee pensions), and 457(b) accounts. Check with the IRS.gov website, or Google "catch-up contributions" for details, but I strongly advise those who are behind on their savings to take advantage of this provision. Your future self will thank you later.

## Working Longer?

Most people I talk to want to retire as soon as it is feasible for them to do so, but not everyone. Some choose to work longer. With some, it is an emotional decision. They love what they do. To them, going to work is not an arduous task, it is like having fun. They love what they do and it is a part of them. They can't see ever letting go of it. I admire and respect that. As a financial advisor, once I find out that is how a client feels, I say put the pedal to the metal and enjoy it!

For some, working longer is purely a financial decision. Several factors go into extending their working life. For one thing, we are living longer lives. This isn't our grandparent's retirement era. Statistics say we are living longer. With an average healthy couple, if one of them makes it to age 65, there is a 23 percent chance that one of them will make it to age 100! Retirements of 20 or 30 years, which were once unheard of, are now distinct possibilities. When it comes to having enough to last the rest of your life, working one extra year buys you *two years* in retirement. That can add up quickly. If one is willing and able to continue working and they wish to make that trade-off, then I say well and good. After all, your greatest asset is not your bank account, or your 401(k). It's your health and your ability to earn income.

Look at all the things that can affect your income 20-30 years down the road. Inflation, taxes, health care, longevity and Social Security. These are all wild cards — X ... the unknown. We really don't know what will happen in those areas. A brochure we hand to all our clients free upon request is titled "Will You Have Enough Income in Retirement?" It helps people, especially those in their 50s, start thinking in that direction so they will be prepared.

# CHAPTER FOUR

# Gross Benefit vs. Net Benefit

"If you wait until you can do everything for everybody instead of something for somebody, you'll end up not doing anything for anybody."

~ Malcolm Bane

W hen was the last time you gave financially to something that you believed in? Making monetary donations, even to a worthy cause, sometimes takes a leap of faith. I have a great friend — a spiritual coach and mentor — who says once you get over the hurdle of making your mind up that you are going to first pay back to God a portion of your income as a gesture of appreciation and thanks for all with which you have been blessed, the next question is how much. The popular term for such giving is tithing, which means giving a tenth.

"So, are you going to tithe on the gross income, or tithe on the net income?" asked my friend.

"What do you suggest?" I replied. And I love what came next.

"I suppose it depends on whether you want the gross blessing or the net blessing in return."

I have read several financial books, and heard many talks from speakers about financial planning. Nearly always, they put forth the opinion that you should always pay yourself first. It has almost become a cliché. There is some merit to that sentiment. I'm sure what they mean is, before you squander your paycheck on frivolous expenditures, set money aside in savings. But every time I hear it, or see it in print, I wonder if the idea of paying oneself first eliminates the idea of first paying *back*.

I don't want to go too religious here, but I know for a fact that the success I have had, and the success our family firm has seen, and the many blessings my wife and I have received through our careers is directly connected with the discipline of paying God first, then saving. In that order. It is up to each individual to decide what that means, of course. Paying God first can mean supporting what charity or ministry you wholeheartedly believe is deserving. I'm not talking about sending a blank check to the money preacher who comes on TV at 3 a.m. I'm talking about an established ministry or charity you believe is doing good works in your community or throughout the world. Our family could not be more pleased with the commitment we made many years ago to the concept of paying God first, and then paying ourselves. If you are a person of faith, you know what I mean. If not, then I leave it there for you to consider.

## Paying Yourself

Now let's get serious about paying yourself.

If you have signed up for a retirement savings plan at work, congratulations. If your employer offers one and you have not signed up for it, we need to talk.

The 401(k) was introduced in the 1980's as more and more companies stopped offering pensions to their employees, because they, the companies, could no longer afford them. Defined-*benefit* plans were replaced by defined-*contribution* plans. This changed the retirement landscape completely. The 401(k) puts the responsibility of retirement into the hands of the individual, not the company.

If you have the opportunity to participate in an employer-sponsored retirement plan that's going to give you any sort of match whatsoever and you are not taking advantage of it, I want you to realize right now you are leaving a tremendous amount of money on the table. It doesn't matter what the employer's contribution is. That is free money!

*"A simple fact that is hard to learn is that the time to save money is when you have some."*

*~ Joe Moore*

One young man told me that he couldn't contribute to his 401(k) at work, even though his employer offered a generous 6 percent match.

"Why not?" I asked.

"I can't afford to," he said. "I don't make enough as it is. In fact, I have been working for the company four years, and I need a raise! As soon as I get a raise, maybe then I will start contributing to my 401(k)."

I told him his raise was sitting right in front of him.

"What do you mean?" he said.

"Your employer is offering to give you 6 percent of what you contribute every month. There's your raise."

Would it surprise you to know that 68 percent of working-age people, those between the ages of 25 and 64, do not participate in an employer-sponsored retirement plan? Those are the facts according to an article that appeared in the Personal Finance section of *Forbes* in April 2015.[11]

---

[11] Laura Shin. Forbes. April 9, 2015. "The Retirement Crisis: Why 68% of Americans Aren't Saving in an Employer-Sponsored Plan." http://www.forbes.com/sites/laurashin/2015/04/09/the-retirement-crisis-why-68-of-

We live in a world of instant gratification. Saving is future gratification, and until we develop the mindset of foresight, we will not be able to fully appreciate the value of paying ourselves first. We all have a future self. One day, decades from now, your future self will inherit the decisions your now self is making, the good ones and the bad ones alike.

## Dollar-Cost Averaging

Timing and persistence are everything when it comes to paying yourself first. An example is the magic of dollar-cost averaging. Let's say you work at XYZ Corporation and, every time you get paid, you make your contribution to your 401(k). It's on autopilot. Without you even thinking about it, the custodians of your retirement plan invest the money for you. How? By buying shares of mutual funds. The way dollar-cost averaging works, when the market goes down, shares are cheaper. Great! Your contribution buys more shares. When the market goes up, great! Your account gets fatter. Because your contributions are always the same and are made every pay period, you are effectively taking advantage of the volatility of the market over time. Your account rises with the tide of the market on an upswing and acquires more shares in a downturn.

Paying oneself first comes down to mindset. Pretend the money you are saving doesn't exist. If you don't see it, you won't spend it. If you make up your mind that way, you won't miss it. It will pour steadily into your account and do its work unseen without your having to do a thing. And no, I'm not saying that you should default on your car payment to pay yourself. Of course you need to stay current on your bills and obligations. But I will say that most people who have difficulty employing this basic principle of money

americans-arent-saving-in-an-employer-sponsored-plan/#603ecbbe19d8. Accessed Feb. 13, 2017.

management aren't acquainted with one specific word. It's the **B** word — with a capital **B** as in Bravo. **A BUDGET!**

As soon they hear the **B** word, some shrink in fear, or run to get two sticks to hold together in the shape of a cross to ward off the evil vampire. But if you are having trouble paying yourself first (saving what you should), a budget is the best gift you could give your future self who will one day thank you.

I can see some of you shaking your head right now, saying this doesn't apply to you. That may be true right now. Maybe you are earning a lot of money. And maybe you don't have to live on a tight budget. I mean, there are some months when there's a little less in the old bank account, and some months when there's a little more. But on the whole, you are not having to dip into savings, or rack up debt on your credit cards to get by. But, at the same time, you probably don't have a grasp of how much you could be saving if you had a budget. I watch people retire every single day of the week, and I am here to tell you that when the paycheck stops, and they begin living off nonrenewable resources, budgeting becomes crucial. Why? Because whether you need \$2,000 a month or \$12,000 a month, you are living on a fixed income. You have this pot of money that is only going to last for so long, and when it's gone, it's gone!

That leads me to the three most important words in retirement. Are you ready? *Income, income, income!*

## *Reverse* Dollar-Cost Averaging

A few paragraphs ago, we talked about dollar-cost averaging and how it protects younger investors during their working years. Well, ironically, the reverse of that same concept can come back to haunt you when you move from the accumulation phase of your financial life to the preservation and distribution phase. Call it *reverse* dollar-cost averaging.

Say you leave XYZ Corporation and you stopped contributing to your 401(k). In fact, the money river is now flowing the other way. Instead of *contributing* to your retirement plan, you are now making *withdrawals* from it to replace the paycheck you used to receive. Because your expenses are constant, you are making those withdrawals with the same regularity with which you used to contribute. You are no longer buying shares; you are selling them with each withdrawal. When share prices go up, you sell fewer shares. If the share prices go down, you sell more shares. You are depleting the account at a faster rate, and every share you sell is one less share that will be working for you in the account. Either way, you are depleting a nonrenewable resource. If the market crashes, the value of your account goes down dramatically and it may take a long time to recoup those losses. This is the most glaringly obvious reason I can cite for rolling over your 401(k) into a self-directed IRA as soon as you retire. Rollovers mean, of course, that the money inside your account does not see your bank account, but slides from one qualified account into another, thus keeping its tax-deferred status without incurring a penalty or creating a taxable event.

A little later in this book we will talk about how you can take everything you have worked so long and hard to accumulate, everything you have sacrificed for, and turn it into an income workhorse down the road. Not just an income workhorse, but a portfolio that can provide you with a powerful tax-free income if you adopt the right strategies.

## Don't Set Your 401(k) Investments on Autopilot

Putting your *contributions* into your 401(k) is fine, but a mistake some individuals make when they are in their 20s, 30s and 40s is failing to stay on top of the investment choices within their retirement plans. When you initially enrolled in your retirement savings plan at work, you were probably overwhelmed with options. You also may have been ill-informed about those choices. How long has it been since you revisited the funds you originally picked? Five years? Ten years? I'm not a mind reader, but I know that most of you reading this right now are still investing in the same mix of

*"If you would be wealthy, think of saving as well as getting."*

*~ Benjamin Franklin*

funds you picked years ago, and when you selected them you probably did so because they were recommended to you as five-star funds. Am I right? The only problem is, every single year that goes by brings an entirely new list of best-performing funds. It is doubtful that you are still in the best-performing funds today.

There is also a pretty good chance you are unaware of new rules and regulations on how and when you can wind down your 401(k) when you are ready to retire. There are also tax implications and potential penalties that can cost you thousands of dollars if you aren't careful with the decisions you will be required to make when you retire.

Finally, let's be honest on this point: there is no rhyme or reason as to how any of the investments inside your 401(k) work with your other retirement accounts or your overall retirement plan. I was working with a younger client recently who had opened a new investment account. He was a conservative investor and wanted to bring some balance to his overall market risk. He also wished to provide his portfolio with some guarantees. This allowed us to look at his Roth 401(k) with an eye toward more aggressive investments. The overall result for this young man will be a greater likelihood for growth. Why? Because we have guaranteed money on the one hand allowing for more aggressive investments on the other. Balance is the key.

If you think risk and reward, often with more risk comes more reward. We want the growth, hopefully the very meaningful growth in that Roth 401(k), and hopefully taking that risk in the Roth 401(k) will enable that growth. An added benefit is that those Roth 401(k) dollars will be tax-free down the road.

It is simply prudent to look at all your accounts regularly and view them as strategic assets. What are they providing you as far as safety, risk and taxes are concerned? Are you going to pay tax on those now, or down the road? Look at your overall portfolio to decide which funds you're picking within that 401(k). Just as puzzle pieces interlock, the pieces of your portfolio need to complement each other and work in harmony.

## Choose Allocations Wisely

The problem with some 401(k)s or 403(b)s is that investment choices can be limited. Some plans offer mutual funds exclusively. Others offer professionally managed accounts of stocks or bonds. Still others may allow you to select from an array of options — company stock, individual stocks, bonds or even variable annuities.

I see a lot of IBM clients. I also deal with quite a few clients who work for Exxon Mobil, BP and 3M Corporation. Many of these individuals have been with these big corporations for 25 years or more and are very loyal employees. Some of them have been given stock options through the years. Company loyalty is fine, but I usually issue a word of caution in this regard. If you have a lot of company stock in your 401(k), it can be hazardous to your wealth. Before you know it, you might have an unbalanced portfolio, putting too much dependence on the performance of one position or one stock. Sometimes, the loyalty factor makes people reluctant to sell out any of their company stock. They feel as if they are going to get into trouble with their employer if they sell any of their company stock. That's why it's better to sit down with a professional who can look at your total investment picture without emotional attachment. Use caution when moving highly appreciated company stock held within a 401(k), or any qualified plan, into an IRA. I see many individuals that have not taken advantage of net unrealized appreciation (NUA) strategies. This can be a costly and irrevocable mistake. Be sure to identify an advisor who is well versed in NUA. From there, work out a plan to balance your portfolio and diversify.

Seek professional advice when selecting allocations within your 401(k). Sit down with a fiduciary advisor who can evaluate your goals. You don't have to be investing your money with this advisor, not if they are a true fiduciary. You should be able to pay them a fee for helping you pick the funds or stocks within the range of investments you are allowed that will perform the best year after year. The fee will likely be far from exorbitant, and the benefits will likely far outweigh the expense.

> *"Many folks think they aren't good at earning money, when what they don't know is how to use it."*
> *~ Frank A. Clark*

Also, I'm not advising you to reallocate quarterly. We're not trying to play the market. I'm just saying that, as you're getting older, your risk level is changing. Typically, you want to be scaling back the risk. Reviewing your allocations every year, or at least every two or three years, is not too frequent. Your portfolio situation may be just fine. If it's not broken, don't fix it, but at least review it.

## The Not-So-Free 401(k)

One more thing while we are on the subject of 401(k)s. They come with costs. Look at the expense ratios on the funds you're picking. While it is true that 401(k)s have gotten better in the last few years, there are still hidden costs in them. Management fees, turnover ratios, expense ratios — all of these must be watched.

Some think they are not paying these fees, since 401(k)s are employer-provided vehicles. Nothing could be further from the truth. You are paying fees that you will not see clearly indicated on your statement. Much of the long-term growth of your retirement savings hinges on your rate of return, and fees attack that rate of return directly. This erosion has a compounding affect.

How can you protect yourself? Look for the expense ratio of the funds you are choosing. The fund is required to disclose the annual fee they charge shareholders.

"What's a percent or two?" said one 401(k) participant.

The answer may surprise you. Just 1 percent translates into thousands of dollars over time. Aim for annual fees closer to 0.1 percent. Mutual funds tend to charge much higher fees. A 2015 Morningstar Report found the average fund within these 401(k)s is charging 1.25 percent. If you just do a little due diligence, maybe seek the help of a professional, you can find some that will charge 0.5 percent or as little as 0.1 percent. It is really worth looking at.[12] Finally, you don't have to obsess over this. Don't let choosing your investments become a do-or-die process that keeps you from making any decisions at all. The important thing is to pay attention to it and diversify as much as possible. I know some people who are so averse to this they don't even open their 401(k) statements and

---

[12] Brett Carson. U.S. News & World Report. March 4, 2015. "The Mutual Fund Fees We Don't Talk About." http://money.usnews.com/money/blogs/the-smarter-mutual-fund-investor/2015/03/04/the-mutual-fund-fees-we-dont-talk-about. Accessed Feb. 13, 2017.

look at them, let alone analyze them to see how much they are paying in fees or see if their investment choices are up to date. All I'm saying is that by putting forth a little time and effort today, you can not only boost your returns, you can give yourself peace of mind going forward. If you aren't doing it already, why not develop the habit of going online regularly to check your 401(k)'s vital signs? Talk to your human resources representative and ask questions. Seek the help of a trusted financial advisor. Your future self will someday walk up to you (hopefully as you are lounging on a sun-splashed beach, while you are sipping a cool drink through a straw from a coconut) and will enthusiastically shake your hand and profusely thank you for displaying such wisdom and good judgment when you were younger.

# CHAPTER FIVE

# Choose What You Love to Do

"Find a job you enjoy doing, and you will never have to work a day in your life."

~ Mark Twain

To give you a little background on my story, and where I've come from, I spent my early years touring the world as a professional musician. They were exciting and exhilarating times. Entertaining thousands of people in a giant arena, I was living out a childhood dream. Night after night in front of cheering crowds, playing music, working with managers to negotiate contracts, I was doing what I loved. In all that time I was wise enough to know that even this season would someday change.

I can't tell you how many nights I went to bed after a big show and lay my head down on a pillow in some hotel room without even knowing what city I was in. I didn't even know what time I had to get on a plane the next morning. A manager always handled those details. There were many late nights, and on each of them, I thanked God for what I considered His blessing — I had landed on the path I had so tirelessly rehearsed to be on and for which I had invested so much blood, sweat and tears to achieve.

I remember walking out onto a stage, knowing it would be one of the last shows of my music career. I was in Sydney, Australia. It was a sold-out arena. The band was doing a big live video shoot. It occurred to me at that moment that here I was, at such a young age, having achieved so much success in an industry that is, I believe, one of the most unfair and challenging industries, saying to myself, "Okay, Chris, what's next? If you're not chasing dollars, fame, guitars and the lifestyle that went with it all, what's next?"

The thing is, I knew what was next. I wasn't blind on where I was headed. Our retirement firm is a family firm. It has been in Central Texas for many, many years. Through years of dinners and holidays and discussions around the table, it was subliminally impressed upon me. I always knew my path was going to land within the financial and retirement planning profession. What I was really asking myself was, would I be able to find the same passion in this new chapter of life that I had for rock 'n' roll? Would I continue to grow and achieve success in this new venture as I had as a touring music artist?

What a quantum leap — going from performing music on stage to helping people pursue their financial dreams and moving from their workaday world into retirement!

My journey in the music industry didn't end due to lack of talent, ambition or connections. It was a personal decision. For one thing, it was just time. I knew I wanted to be a father who was there for his kids. I knew how quickly, like the blink of an eye, that precious time would pass. I wanted to be there for all of it. I wanted to spend time with my wife, too. Touring the world didn't allow for either of those. I must tell you, looking back, being a husband and a father is the best gig in the world, and opting for it was the best decision I ever made. I could navigate and find my niche and status in the financial services industry here in Central Texas and pursue another passion for my daily work. I consider myself to be truly fortunate indeed, and hope I will continue to do that for the rest of my life.

If you are in a job that makes you miserable, it is not worth it. If you are driving to work dreading every mile that brings you closer to the office, and you find yourself waking up every morning cursing the dawn, then it's time to reconsider what you are doing and why. Time is everything. The time from your 20s to your 50s is your most productive. If you don't have a passion for what you are doing, or if you cannot *find* a passion for it, then you will limit your potential for growth as well as your earnings potential. At some point, you will stop striving for success and compromise your quality of life. That will have a ripple effect on those around you. It will also affect the quality of life of your spouse, your children, and possibly even your grandchildren. If you are merely punching the clock and living just for the weekend, and counting down the hours until it comes, there is a good chance you're not doing something you care about. Life's too short for that.

Try to find that passion. It could be within the same job, or the same company. Perhaps a different role, a different position. Find a way to merge your passion in some form in your professional life. Let's be real. The truth is, most people out there aren't going to find their dream job. Many people don't even know what their dream job is. It could also be that you have tried a couple of things that just didn't work out. You could try looking within your situation. Look where you're at, in other words. Find a way to bring more value through your passion to what you are doing daily.

One of my favorite stories having to do with this involves a man who came across three masons who were hard at work. They were chipping away at a large block of granite. The first mason was obviously unhappy at his job. He kept looking at his watch. The observer asked him what he was doing.

"I'm hammering on this rock," he replied with a growl. "What does it look like?" He added that, as soon as the clock struck five, he was headed home.

The second worker seemed in a better frame of mind. When the man asked him what he was doing, he said, "I'm preparing this stone to be part of a wall I'm building. I'll be glad when it's finished, but it's not bad work."

The third mason, however, was chiseling diligently, occasionally stepping back to inspect and admire his work. When the man asked him what he was doing, the third worker replied, "Why, I'm building a cathedral that will probably last for centuries and allow families of people I will never know to enter here and worship God."

*The biggest mistake you can make is to believe you are working for somebody else.*

*The driving force of a career must come from the individual.*

*Remember: jobs are owned by a company, but YOU own your CAREER.*

All three men were doing the same job. They just had different attitudes toward the job they were doing.

How well that illustrates what a difference our attitude can make. It can transform how we approach our job, the quality of the work we do, and can make even the most laborious task a cheerful pleasure. That spirit spreads to everyone around us, too.

# CHAPTER SIX

# Monumental Gen-X and Gen-Y Mistakes

"They say genes skip a generation. Maybe that's why grandparents find their grandchildren so likable."

~ Joan McIntosh

So, at 6:30 a.m. one Monday in Austin, I'm behind the microphone in the studio of a news radio station, going over the latest world events. Every week we talk about current events and how they affect the market.

That week, a big employment report had just been released. Unemployment was down to 4.9 percent — the lowest it had been since 2008. But for some reason, the market was not responding positively to the news. Why was that? Because the numbers were deceiving. Yes, more people were working. Yes, fewer people who had lost jobs were accepting unemployment compensation, but that didn't tell the entire story. Behind the glamorous news headline lay the ugly fact that middle-class Americans, after you adjust for inflation, were earning no more today than they did 20 years ago. That means they weren't getting ahead. They were just getting by.

Later on that day, between appointments, I began thinking about people I know who have successful businesses, some who get nice yearly raises and promotions, but still fall into the category of what I call "the high-earning poor." On the surface, they may not look broke. Based on their clothes or the cars they drive, they may even appear prosperous. But if you looked at their balance sheet, you would see they are living paycheck to paycheck.

> *"Many people take no care of their money till they come nearly to the end of it and others do just the same with their time."*
> *~ Johann Wolfgang von Goethe*

The crazy thing is, this is, I suspect, a large segment of the population. They have a nice income, but they are asset poor. And it is all a matter of money management. These individuals have no emergency fund whatsoever. A financial emergency would sink their ship in a hurry. They have no retirement to speak of because it takes all they earn just to maintain their lifestyle.

Many consider $70,000 to be at the high end of the salary range in America today. Yet, with an average house in an average neighborhood with two cars, two kids and a mortgage, that is a tough number on which to get by, much less salt money away for your golden years.

Would it surprise you to learn that I know people who are earning double and triple $70,000 per year who still live from paycheck to paycheck **and** are saddled with oppressive debt? Well, it's true.

I believe there are a couple of reasons for this. One is the 401(k) plans introduced back in the 1980s have become the pillar of most people's savings. That's great, but the problem is that, after putting money into these retirement plans, people don't have any left over. They can't touch these accounts (without penalty) until they reach 59 ½, which means they are locking up money. And they don't have much left over for savings or for emergencies.

The emergency account should be flush for when we get into a pinch. It should be the reserve we use to keep us from tapping our savings, or going into debt, which is worse. A good rule of thumb is to have at least six months' income (I prefer nine months) for the unexpected during your working years. A car breaks down. The roof needs replacing. An illness or accident interrupts your flow of income. It is just basic financial planning to have such a fund. The emergency fund needs to be liquid. If you can put the money to work for you, well and good, but you need to be able to write a check or visit an automatic teller machine (ATM) and obtain cash in an instant.

What I learn when I talk with Gen Xers (those born in the late 1960s and 1970s) and those of Generation Y (those born in the 1980s and 1990s) is that very few of them have such a fund set aside. For those in Generation Y, retirement is a far distant horizon. Most of this age group are so plugged into today that tomorrow doesn't appear real to them. Gen Xers are a little better in this regard.

I also note that, in some, there is almost a sense of entitlement. Many of them are college graduates who feel they spent all those years studying, so they must have the new S600 Mercedes or the house with a three-car garage and a swimming pool. Some find themselves up to their eyeballs in college debt, car payments and mortgages. They live in a much bigger house than they need, or opt for a downtown condo with an extra-large patio and a view of the Capitol, which can be just as expensive. But some of these individuals are "successful" by the accepted definition, whether we're talking about the 37-year-old who has his own business that's rocking, or the 42-year-old physician with his own practice. They have "good money" coming in, but it is going out as fast as it comes in and they have little to show for it.

I saw an interesting bumper sticker the other day: "Whoever dies with the most toys wins." It speaks to the futility of amassing stuff at the expense of planning for a purposeful and comfortably lived future. Like the adage says: "If your income exceeds your outgo then your upkeep will be your downfall."

If all the money you earn is going out, and you have little in liquid savings, the danger is obvious. If you lose your job, there's no cushion there to ensure you can still pay that mortgage or car payment. What are you going to tap into? You will tap into whatever savings you have. Or you will go to your retirement account and in the process get smacked with high taxes and penalties.

If you are successful, you are probably in at least a tax bracket of 25 percent or higher. If you are extremely successful, you will be paying 39.5 percent in taxes or more. When you pull money out of your retirement account, it is counted as earned income. If you are under 59 ½, there goes another 10 percent off the top! In some cases, you have a 60-day window to pay the money back to the same IRA from which it was withdrawn and avoid the penalty. The problem is, most people never pay it back, even if they intend to.

> *"Money is only a tool. It will take you wherever you wish, but it will not replace you as the driver."*
> *~ Ayn Rand*

## Not Participating in 401(k)

If you are in your 20s, 30s and 40s staying on top of your 401(k) allocations can absolutely save you thousands of dollars over your working career.

If you signed up for a 401(k), you are to be commended! You did a smart thing. The findings of a Schwartz Center for Economic Policy Analysis survey were reported in an April 9, 2015 *Forbes* article, "The Retirement Crisis: Why 68% Of Americans Aren't Saving In An Employer-Sponsored Plan." The headline says it all. What are they thinking? That Social Security will be enough to carry them through? For the youngest of the bunch, there is no guarantee Social Security will even be around by the time they retire. If it is, it may be a much-diminished version of what it is today.[13]

The article pointed out that almost half of working Americans are not offered retirement plans by their employers. Yet an alarming number are offered a plan and simply refuse to participate — even if the employer is offering matching funds. As I have said earlier in this book, if your employer is offering matching funds, that is *free money!* Jump on it.

## Young Investors Should Embrace Risk

You have probably heard of the Investing Rule of 100. Take your age and subtract it from 100. That's how much of your assets you should have at risk. The rest should be safe. Some shorten it to simply putting a percent sign after your age. That figure represents

---

[13] Laura Shin. Forbes. April 9, 2015. "The Retirement Crisis: Why 68% of Americans Aren't Saving in an Employer-Sponsored Plan." http://www.forbes.com/sites/laurashin/2015/04/09/the-retirement-crisis-why-68-of-americans-arent-saving-in-an-employer-sponsored-plan/#603ecbbe19d8. Accessed Feb. 13, 2017.

the percentage of your assets that you should keep protected from loss.

That means if you are 25, 75 percent of your assets should be aggressively invested and 25 percent should be safe — probably in a healthy emergency fund. This will vary, of course, if you are one of the lucky few who has a pension, or some other substantial source of guaranteed income.

I had a client in his early 30s show up the other day. We discussed his 401(k) allocations. He saw his father lose nearly half of his retirement savings in the 2008 financial crisis, and this influenced his thinking. He was ultra conservative. He had moved nearly all his 401(k) to money market funds, which is the same as cash. The only problem with that is they weren't growing.

The younger Gen Xers and those of Generation Y have seen the tech wreck of 2001 and the Great Recession of 2008. I can understand their being apprehensive about putting a lot of money in the stock market. They don't want to see what they have worked so hard to acquire go down the drain. They reason, "The markets have recovered, but all it takes is a little political hiccup on the other side of the world, like the United Kingdom exiting the European Union, to send the market into a tailspin. With the markets that volatile, maybe I should just park my money on the sidelines, and just prepare to weather the storm."

If you are reading this book and you are over the age of 50, I agree with that kind of thinking. You are, after all, getting closer to the time in your life when you need to preserve your assets. But if you are in your 30s and 40s, you are still in your accumulation years. You should put as much as you can into your savings plan and invest somewhat aggressively. You have time on your side. Economic downturns are called corrections for a reason. The market dips, sometimes severely, but it has always rebounded. TIME is the key factor. I don't care how sizable your retirement or savings accounts are, your TIME and your health are the greatest assets you have! If the recovery period is long and drawn out and you are in your 50s and 60s, you may not have time to recoup your losses. But if you are in your 20s, 30s and 40s, you almost certainly will have time. When you are in "accumulation mode," you need to pack in as much into your coffers as possible. Invest in it on a regular basis — at least monthly. Then, when you get in your 50s and 60s, it's all about preserving what you've got. Taking chips off the table so when you retire you will have the resources you need. Think about it. If you were investing into your 401(k) in 2008, losing only 5-10 percent in that account would have been considered a minor miracle, right? But what I see is a 5-10 percent correction gets people's attention fast. It makes them think about their risk tolerance. That's a good thing because it makes investors re-evaluate where they are.

Investors with $100,000 to $200,000 in their portfolios lost an average of 21 percent during the 2008 financial crisis, while those with more than $200,000 lost an average of 25 percent. But the averages of course don't tell the whole story — some investors lost as much as half of their retirement savings.[14] It all depended on their level of exposure. It happened so quickly that it scarred some investors, to the point that when they see a 5-10 percent correction, which is normal market behavior, they get that sinking feeling in the pits of their stomachs, thinking it's 2008 or 2001 all over again. I'm not faulting people for that, but what I want to get across is, if you are between the ages of 20 and 50, there is no need to panic. You have time on your side. This is especially the case if you are steadily contributing to a 401(k)-type plan. You must realize any investment will have ups and downs, good days and bad days. If you have committed to a monthly contribution, then dollar-cost

---

[14] Emily Brandon and Katy Marquardt. U.S. News & World Report. Feb. 12, 2009. "How Did Your 401(k) Really Stack Up in 2008?" http://money.usnews.com/money/retirement/articles/2009/02/12/how-did-your-401k-really-stack-up-in-2008. Accessed Feb. 7, 2017.

averaging will help you — if you keep putting in the same amount each month, increasing your contributions if you can.

Of course, it's never fun to see money evaporate when the market is falling, even for a 20- or 30-year-old, but they can rejoice in the knowledge that their investment dollar has more purchasing power on a down cycle. Know those skinny shares will fatten back up in time.

A key to a healthy 401(k) is balancing the funds annually. Whatever you do, don't start looking at your account every day. There are several reasons for this. First, it won't give you the true picture. It's like looking at a television screen from two inches away. All you will see are a bunch of colored pixels — not the big picture. Secondly, you are too busy for that. If you are a young investor, you're probably raising a family along with working hard and building a career. Go do that. You need to be having your morning meditation, not staring at a stock market ticker and studying the symbols. Put confidence in dollar-cost averaging and continue investing through thick and thin, up and down. Evening things out over time can allow you to stay on track toward your retirement goal.

> "Money is a terrible master but an excellent servant."
> ~ P.T. Barnum

## Saving Only in Your 401(k)

Another classic mistake I see Gen Xers and millennials make is limiting their savings to their employer-sponsored retirement plans. Why is this? Is it because this is what they see others doing? They call it herd mentality. Lemmings are those furry little hamster-like rodents that, for some strange reason, occasionally run en masse off cliffs into the sea. Young investors sometimes exhibit the same behavior, following the herd, and this is a big problem. Some just do what they did last week because it's all they know how to do. If you are one of those, give yourself a little checkup from the neck up and do a little creative thinking.

Your 401(k) or 403(b) is great, but there are many different options out there. If you are a younger saver and investor, and your 401(k) is your only savings focus, you are putting all your money into a bucket you can't touch for 20-30 years. There are a few exceptions to this, but you generally can't access money in tax-deferred retirement savings plans without facing hefty penalties until you are 59 ½ years old, based on

*"You must gain control over your money or the lack of it will forever control you."*

*~ Dave Ramsey*

tax laws in existence when this book was written. So, if you are 25, 30, 35 years old, and contributing the maximum, at current contribution limits for those under 50, you are putting in approximately $18,000 a year. You are probably pleased with yourself. "I'm just loading this thing up," you say to yourself, but you are locking it up, too. Don't forget that.

If you do your own taxes, you are probably very excited when you see how much money you're saving in taxes by contributing to your 401(k). Depending on your income, each contribution could be a deduction. You look at it as a win/win situation. You get to shave that much off of your reportable income and you get to keep the money, albeit with a few access restrictions, and watch it grow.

Or, if you have a certified public accountant, or CPA, do your taxes, he or she is pleased to see your contributions to a tax-deferred retirement savings plan. After all, you are paying your CPA to limit your tax exposure and find as many deductions (and as large a refund) as possible. Your CPA may even tell you to pay as little in the way of taxes now, while you're in a high-income bracket, and pay them later down the road when you retire.

By the way, I'm not picking on CPAs, here. I work with three or four tremendous CPAs to whom we send our clients. I know them well and respect them. What I am talking about here is the mentality I believe most people have — trying to save a penny today, without much thought to the long-term results of the action. Remember, you are participating in a *tax-deferred* savings plan, not a *tax-free* savings plan. It is on this subject that I am trying to educate younger savers and investors. I know of several people in their 30s who are making mid-six figures. True, they may be giving ole Uncle Sam's IRS the stiff-arm now, but those chickens will come home to roost later. Because, bear in mind, that money you are paying into your 401(k) will be growing over the next 20-30 years. You will pay taxes on a much larger sum.

## Pay Tax on the Seed or the Harvest

Think of tax deferral this way. You are a farmer. You go into the feed and seed store in the spring to buy seed for planting. As you are at the counter, a tall man with a gray goatee wearing a top hat and a stars-and-stripes suit comes up to you. Yes, it's Uncle Sam.

"Howdy, partner," he says. "I have a proposition for you."

"What is it?" you reply.

"You can pay taxes on that seed now and be done with it, or you can pay taxes on the harvest later," Uncle Sam says.

Would you take the deal? Probably not. Paying taxes on the harvest would be a much larger amount. And yet, that is exactly what tax deferral amounts to. That's why Roth IRAs and Roth 401(k)s are becoming more and more popular. With them, you pay the tax on the front end and get it over with. Then your investment is not taxed as it grows, nor is it taxed when you withdraw it. I have made this point many times in articles I have written for *Forbes* and

*Money Magazine.* Still, the message doesn't seem to filter down to the masses of people just starting out in their careers and launching their saving and investing lives.

One real edge that I have, I believe, is the privilege of working with people of all ages and all walks of life. I have plenty of clients who are retirees, and who are in higher tax brackets when they retire than when they were working. How did that happen? Several factors contribute to it. Many of them become more successful at their careers as time goes by. When they approach retirement years, they can pay off the mortgage on

*"The income tax has made more liars out of the American people than golf has. Even when you make a tax form out on the level, you don't know when it's through if you are a crook or a martyr."*
*~ Will Rogers*

their house — their largest tax deduction. Also, their children grow up and leave home. There go more deductions. If they have been diligent savers and responsible investors, there is a good chance they have amassed a huge 401(k) or a very large IRA. Name the pre-tax account, and they probably have a sizable one, if not two.

Then, they retire. Now they start pulling money from those accounts, and, you guessed it, paying *taxes* with each withdrawal. They are now paying taxes on a very large pot of money that they have never paid a dime of taxes on.

Let's say you are fortunate enough to have some royalty income, and let's say you are fortunate enough to be one of the few who has a pension. Couple that with taxable Social Security, and it is easy to see how some people will pay much more in taxes in retirement than they would have dreamed of in their 30s.

## Required Minimum Distributions

Let's say you are retired and you don't need to take money out of your 401(k). You could just let it sit on the sidelines and continue to grow. It comes as a surprise to some when they learn at age 70 ½, the government requires you to take at least a minimum amount from your account, or RMDs for shorthand (required minimum distributions). In other words, you are forced to withdraw a portion of the money in the account each year commensurate with your age, per the government's life expectancy tables.

I have many couples as clients who are in higher tax brackets when they retire. They have more than enough income to see them through without tapping their retirement savings accounts. But then, when they reach their 70s, Uncle Sam comes knocking and they have to pull out their checkbook and make a withdrawal they would rather not make, and pay taxes on it. Even more disconcerting? The amount they are forced to withdraw goes up every year. There is a very good chance the income they are forced to pull out could put them in a higher tax bracket. When you jump to higher tax brackets, it often means your Social Security will be taxed at a higher rate and your Medicare premiums will go up. So, it tends to have a snowball effect.

*"It's not how much money you make, but how much money you keep, how hard it works for you and how many generations you keep it for."*

*~ Robert Kiyosaki*

So, if you are dumping ALL your money into tax-deferred savings such as IRAs and 401(k)s, you may be inadvertently setting yourself up to be taxed on the harvest — the bigger number — than the seed. I am used to paying 10 cents on every dollar I make. Yes, it is painful to even think about. The truly scary thing is, as I write this book, we are near historically low tax rates. But we also have, like the sword of Damocles hanging above our necks, a $19 trillion (and rising as I write this) national debt. The only way that debt can be paid is for the government to tax its citizens more and give them less to show for it. So, where am I going with this? If we are setting ourselves up to be taxed on the larger number down the road and tax rates increase, then we are creating a potential tax bomb. Not to mention — and I must reinforce this — the fact that we are tying up our funds. Meanwhile, life goes on. There will be weddings to pay for, homes to buy and furnish, college educations to fund. All sorts of expenses that will never stop coming.

As we are mapping out where and how to save for the future, we need to be looking at 401(k)s and IRAs. I am by no means against these pre-taxed retirement accounts, but you will want to have balance in your portfolio — some pre-tax accounts, some post-tax accounts, some nonqualified accounts.

Think about tax diversification, too. The easiest way to think about it is this: if you, let's say, need $75,000 income in retirement, and $40,000 is covered through Social Security and maybe a small pension or some royalty income, from what source will you pull the other $35,000?

"Well, I'll go to my 401(k)," you may say.

Let's say you withdraw $25,000 from your 401(k). Now you are approaching a higher tax bracket, and you still need another $10,000 to make the $75,000 budget. If that's the only bucket you have to go to, you are forced to make a withdrawal that will jump you into a higher tax bracket. But if you have some nonqualified account, or, even better, a Roth IRA, Roth 401(k) or even a health savings account (HSA), then the tax problem may be avoided.

HSA money can be a very valuable tool in your toolbox. In the above scenario, it could be a good place from which to withdraw the additional $10,000 to make our $75,000 budget. Money that comes out of HSAs for medical expenses does not create a taxable event. Plus, once you have reached age 65, you can withdraw funds from your HSA for any purpose without penalty and will only pay income tax on your withdrawal. Additionally, while distributions will be subject to income taxes, you can pass your HSA funds on, estate-tax-free, to your beneficiaries.

Using a Roth account to fund the additional $10,000 in the preceding illustration would also work since funds you take from Roth accounts do not create a taxable event. Why? For Roth accounts, the taxes have already been paid when the money went into the account. On top of that, you were able to see the money growing over the years, and you never paid a dime in taxes on the gains. In this scenario, when you turn 70 ½, there are no RMDs to deal with. Then, based on today's tax code, when you pass away, you leave every dollar and every cent to your family, your beneficiaries, your kids, your heirs, whomever they may be, 100 percent tax free.

# CHAPTER SEVEN

# Scout Out Wisdom

"Knowledge comes from learning. Wisdom comes from living."
~ Anthony Douglas Williams

My grandfather on my mother's side was the Rev. Don Powell. He was an evangelist who preached all over the world in the 1950s and 1960s. He also owned a Christian Gospel radio station in Upton, Kentucky. He once told me, "Knowledge is having a collection of facts in your head," he said. "If you know a train is coming down the tracks, that is knowledge. If you know you are standing on the railroad track, that is knowledge."

"Wisdom is putting the two things together and acting on it," he said. "Getting off the tracks, in other words."

There are many things out there that will sabotage your success if you don't understand them and act on what you know. It seems I have spent my whole life associating with people who were older than me. Even my best friend in elementary school was a couple of grades higher than me. The age difference didn't matter to me at all. Growing up, I learned a lot from him.

In my teens, one of my closest friends was 10 years older than me. He was married. He had a job. He had bills. I remember thinking, "I could learn from that."

When I was in my 20s, one of my closest friends was someone I toured with, and again, he was around 10 years older than me. That 10-year chasm is huge during that phase of life, I realize, but I was eager to learn from him as well. To this day, my closest friends have a good five to 15 years on me. I can tell you this with confidence: there is much to be gained by associating yourself with people who are older than you.

Conversely, continuous association with those who have less experience than you, and do not share your goals, can be counterproductive. In some cases, hanging out with the wrong crowd can send you into a nosedive. When you surround yourself with talented, driven people who have a little bit more knowledge, a little bit more life experience than you, a little bit of that rubs off on you, making you a better person.

If you are going to hang out with people your own age, that's fine, but they need to be on your level. I'm not necessarily talking about on your level as far as income and education, but it will benefit you if you invest your time and energy in people who uplift you and have something to contribute. It is true, however, that people who have money tend to make friends with others who have money. That's just the way it is.

I've had an individual in my life through the years with whom I never was personally in business, but when we would get together, I would bounce ideas off him. He was wise. But he was also fearful to take any risk at all. He didn't like anything new. It was uncomfortable for him. He owned a business, and from time to time I would try to help him with it. But every suggestion I made was just outside his comfort zone, or just a little too risky. The suggestion just wasn't, to put it in his words, "organic enough."

I learned something from this relationship. If you are too close-minded, you will seldom get ahead in your endeavors. If you cannot and will not imagine and create and collaborate with others on ideas and ways to grow yourself in your personal or professional life, then you will remain where you are. I'm not sure Albert Einstein is the one who said it, but the words are credited to him: "The definition of insanity is doing the same thing over and over and expecting different results."

Are you able to work with people? Are you one of those who goes from job to job, and you've had at least six of them in the last five years, and it's always someone else's fault when you leave or are fired? It's always your boss who was too hard on you. Maybe the staff was cliquish and they wouldn't let you in the club? Perhaps

your boss was too demanding, making you work too late. Ask yourself: "Am I able to work with others?"

I believe the main reason why people lose in life — whether it's a job title, a role or a big opportunity — is their inability to work, communicate and mesh with other people. It's such a big part of life. It works out so much better to get into an environment and go with the flow. Bring value to whatever undertaking with which you find yourself involved, and do so to the point where you stand out in the crowd. Not that you are showboating or putting others down, but your character is revealed when you show yourself to be confident in who you are and the purpose for which you are working.

# CHAPTER EIGHT

# The Paycheck Isn't the Path to Wealth

"A good job is more than just a paycheck. A good job fosters independence and discipline, and contributes to the health of the community. A good job is a means to provide for the health and welfare of your family, to own a home, and save for retirement."

~ James H. Douglas Jr.

You are in your 20s, 30s or 40s and you are trying to land that job. Trying to win that new position. What is the driver there? Is it the job title? Is it the bigger office? Is it the company car, or some other perk that comes with the next rung up the ladder? Or is it the prestige of a more impressive title on your business card? I don't think it's any of that. Not really. When the dust settles and the smoke clears, it's the paycheck.

I think, as we climb the ladder of success, we tend to hang our identity and our financial security on our position or title at work. Maybe we think it's about our relationship with a corporation that shows us they value our service and the talent we bring to the company. At the end of the day, we wouldn't be interested in any of those things if they didn't pay us. Society tells us the more we earn, the better off we will be. The more you make, the wealthier you are. Baseball is not the great American pastime; chasing the paycheck is.

But if you think chasing a paycheck is going to make you wealthy, you are dead wrong. Here's why:

Pay raises are never in big lump sums, they are in nickels and dimes. Typically, you just don't go from a $35,000 a year job to a $65,000 a year job and you don't go from a $65,000 per year job to a $150,000 per year job. It just doesn't happen that way for most people.

At REAP Financial, I work with a lot of small business owners. It is not uncommon for them to have a dead year, a flat year. A year when they are barely making payroll. Then the following year, they may be able to pay themselves $1.5 million, and they come to my office and say, "What should I do with this?"

> *"The habit of saving is itself an education, it fosters every virtue, teaches self-denial, cultivates the sense of order, trains to forethought and so broadens the mind."*
> ~ T.T. Munger

But for those who work for a corporation, they may get a small bump in their pay here and there with small promotions. Usually the increase in income comes with a small promotion or a new job title, or both. When this happens, their lifestyle gets a bump as well. What usually follows these raises in pay is an expansion of the recipient's lifestyle. It always seems to follow that when the person earns more, they feel obliged to spend more on the way they live. There is a sense of entitlement. "Lord knows," they tell themselves, "I've earned it. I have worked hard for it, and now I'm going to enjoy it."

This attitude toward the paycheck is especially embraced by most millennials I have met — those of what I call the "younger generation." So if the paycheck won't make you rich, what will?

- Living below your means
- Aggressively saving
- Disciplined investing

Many millennials and Gen Xers are savers; they just don't save enough. Few of them are investors. The kind of saving the younger generation seems to engage in is the kind that allows them access to their money. Liquidity is a wonderful thing, but when it comes to investing, you must sacrifice a measure of liquidity to obtain the kind of returns that make it profitable. That's why CDs and money market funds, both extremely liquid investments, offer such paltry returns (usually a fraction of a percent).

Many of the younger generation don't trust investing. They saw their parents get beat up in the stock market crashes and corrections of the 2000s. They have witnessed the volatility of the stock market in the changing economic climate during the first 15 years of the 21st century.

Here in Austin, the banks are offering such low rates of interest they don't even keep up with inflation. And if you don't think inflation is alive and well, come to Austin. In Central Texas (and I'm sure this area isn't the only section of the country dealing with this) property taxes are out of control. When you walk out of the grocery store with two bags of groceries, you have usually spent $75 to $100 for what you can carry in with two hands. Twenty years ago, $100 would fill four or five bags. That's inflation.

## That Safe Feeling

We feel safe with our money at the banks, but it's not a long-term play. Bank CDs and savings accounts may be liquid and safe, but your purchasing power in 15 to 18 years will be cut in half — this based on historical inflation rates of 3.31 percent.

"But I like to be safe and conservative," you may say. "That way I can sleep well at night, knowing my assets are protected." What should disturb your rest, at least a little bit, is the fact that you are paying for that safety by exposing yourself to the effects of inflation in the long term.

It is nearly impossible in this day and age to keep your money liquid, and in an investment that keeps ahead of inflation, while at the same time avoiding a lot of risk. This is why I keep beating the drum of alternative investing — putting together a plan that is commensurate with your age and your proximity to retirement. If you are conservative, that's fine. But you must have a portion of your portfolio working for you to offset inflation while the rest remains safe.

*Regardless of what vehicle you put money into, there is a measure of risk. Either the risk of losing in a big stock market downturn, or the risk of being so conservative that you're losing money and purchasing power due to inflation.*

What I tell "low-risk investors," people who don't have the stomach for risk, is every investment, every vehicle that you can put money in, it will carry some type of risk. It is important to understand that fact. Regardless of what vehicle you put money into, there is a measure of risk. Either the risk of losing money in a big stock market downturn, or the risk of being so conservative that you're losing money and purchasing power due to inflation.

I have money in the stock market. My family has money in the stock market. I am securities licensed, and many of my clients have money invested in the stock market, but I am also very cautious.

Although experienced sailors love the sea, they also have a healthy respect for the inherent danger it represents. I, too, have a healthy respect for the stock market, especially in the volatile economic climate that prevails as this book is written. My approach, especially with my clients who are nearing retirement, is very conservative. I focus primarily on preserving the cash they need to retire and maintain their lifestyle. But after that aspect of their financial house — call it the foundation — is in place, a portion of their portfolio needs to be employed, not sitting idle on the sidelines, so they will not be blindsided by inflation.

# CHAPTER NINE

# Help the Kids Now;
# Live With Them Later?

"Every generation thinks it has the answer: and every generation is humbled by nature."

~ Philip Lubin

Generation X was born between 1965 and 1976. There are approximately 51 million Gen Xers living in America. The front edge of this group has now entered their 50s.

Gen Xers grew up during a time when technology was just coming of age. During their formative years, the desktop computer was becoming a household item. They learned hand-eye coordination by playing video games. They are accustomed to instant communication and took fax machines for granted. To them, a cellphone is a given.

Most Generation X households have two earners. Unlike their baby boomer parents, they did not grow up in fear of nuclear annihilation. They never heard the words "duck and cover" in elementary school. The Cold War ended when they were in or around their 20s.

They saw the rapid economic growth of the 1990s, but they were also witness to the collapse of the stock market during the dot-com era, and the 2008 financial crisis, events that continue to affect their financial behavior. According to a 2014 study by the Insured Retirement Institute (IRI), only 65 percent of Gen Xers have money saved for retirement, and not very much at that.

> *"Too many people spend money they haven't earned to buy things they don't want to impress people they don't like."*
>
> *~ Will Rogers*

The average savings for Generation X amounts to just under $60,000. Forty-two percent have less than $50,000 saved up for retirement.[15]

I am convinced the two most common mistakes for Generation X is (a) failing to save, and (b) not seeking the help of financial professionals. According to the IRI survey, those Gen Xers who sought assistance from a financial planner were far better off. "The median amount saved for retirement by Gen Xers who work with a financial planner is $90,400, which is twice the amount saved by Gen Xers who do not work with a financial planner," the survey reported. But it's getting worse, not better. The study confirmed the number of Gen Xers working with financial planners is going down. Seventy-seven percent said they were **not** consulting a financial planner to help them plan for their retirement, whereas in 2012 that number was 63 percent. One-fourth of those surveyed said they have no idea when they plan to retire.

---

[15] Insured Retirement Institute. January 2014. "The Retirement Readiness of Generation X: The Lasting Effects of the 'Great Recession' on Gen-Xers' Retirement Outlook." https://www.myirionline.org/docs/default-source/research/the-retirement-readiness of generation x january 2014. Accessed Feb. 13, 2017.

## Money for College

Most members of Generation X went to college and saw it as a birthright, but that was when it cost far less. Half of Generation X paid less than $10,000 a year for their college education, whereas only 27 percent of their children (millennials) could find universities charging less than $10,000 per year. [16]

But Generation X is bound and determined to send their kids to college, even if it means drastically reducing their retirement security.

I think it's an amazing gift and accomplishment to be able to help your children through school — hopefully without their having to go through their young working years saddled with two decades of debt. But there is no greater financial gift you parents can give your children than *your own* sound and secure retirement. Why is that?

At age 40, it's hard for some people to come to terms with this fact: if their retirement nest egg dwindles and disappears, they will find themselves in a position of possibly moving in with their kids. When you focus the bright spotlight of reality on the financial situation of many Generation X households, that situation is a real possibility. For most people, it is a ghastly thought. Without a little planning now, I'm afraid many Gen Xers will find themselves with little choice in the matter when their tanks run dry, and that's assuming their children are good stewards of their education and become successful to the point where they can afford to take their parents in.

I suppose what drops out the bottom of my calling attention to these ominous but statistically real possibilities is this: seek the help of a financial planner ASAP. I know you love your kids, but it's a

---

[16] Tom Wray. Ion Tuition. July 17, 2015. "News Flash! Survey compares student debt attitudes: Millenials vs. Gen X." https://blog.iontuition.com/news-flash-survey-compares-student-debt-attitudes-millennials-vs-gen-x/. Accessed Feb. 13, 2017.

totally different ball game if you find yourself having to live with them.

Gen Xers are faced with a choice of whether to save aggressively for the college education of their children or save aggressively for retirement. It would be nice if they could do both, but most don't seem to be able to do that. They are watching university tuitions rise higher and higher, while, at the same time, their Social Security appears to be threatened. As options go, it's the proverbial juxtaposition between a rock and a hard place for them. What I see: many parents in this age group are jeopardizing their retirements to help their kids get an education.

When weighing whether to save for the kids' college or save for your own retirement, consider this: it is a sure bet that one day you will stop working and must rely on your savings, your Social Security, and your income from investments to survive. With the kids' college education, there are many unknowns. Will they go to private or public schools? Will they qualify for scholarships? Are there government grants available? Will they be able to help with their tuition by working part-time? Are student loans a viable option? According to college cost researcher Tom Wray:

"Millennials, who were born between 1981 and 2004, see more value in a college degree than Gen Xers and are willing to pay for it. Even with higher costs, millennials still see the value of a four-year degree," Wray says. "When asked if it's worth the price, 76 percent said yes, while 68 percent of Gen X reported the same."[17]

There are several ways to pay for a college education, but putting off saving for retirement can be hazardous to your wealth.

Before I write this next paragraph, let me say that I know I have hammered on this nail before, but it deserves one more strike. If you are married and have a family and don't have an emergency fund, you could be in big trouble if you lose your job, or experience

---

[17] Ibid.

some other unexpected event that could threaten your financial security. Salt away at least six (preferably nine) months liquid savings for emergencies. And don't be penny wise and pound foolish; buy insurance on your life and your home.

## Seeking Financial Advice

I probably don't have to convince anyone reading this book that going to a doctor at least once a year for a physical examination is a good idea and could help you lead a long and healthy life. I don't suppose I need to say that seeing a medical professional when you have an ailment that doesn't seem to want to go away makes far more sense than trying to diagnose the problem yourself.

The sad fact is, however, that most people take far better care of their health than they do their wealth. In my profession, I see many in the 40-something generation making the mistake of not seeking specialized professional financial help. I can understand the 23-year-old, who has little in the way of assets and who is just starting out in life, postponing consulting with a financial planner. That's understandable. There may not be a lot of money coming in. They are trying to get on their feet, get out of college, land a job. They are doing well just paying their cellphone bill. To them, retirement is a far away horizon. But by the time you are 40, chances are you have landed a career and are making money. And you have probably begun to climb the financial ladder. If you have not sought professional help, it may be because you are working your tail off and you have two or three kids at home that occupy every minute of your free time. I get all of that. I'm just saying that seeing a financial counselor in that phase of your life is probably the most valuable move you could possibly make for your family.

I can hear some people now saying, "Hey, if I don't have wealth, why do I need financial help?"

If you have a paycheck coming in, you need a strategy. It doesn't have to be a big, elaborate plan with several moving parts and income streams. But you need a strategy on how and where you are investing your money — even if it's your 401(k).

Most people pick a handful of five-star mutual funds, and set their 401(k) on autopilot and never look at it. But every year brings an entirely new set of five-star mutual funds to the table. I understand the set-it-and-forget it mentality, but here is a golden opportunity to make some small reallocations to take advantage of which funds are performing better than others. If I told you that XYZ fund was underperforming and you could, without cost, move your money into an ABC fund that was going to yield much better results, would you move the funds? Of course you would!

Also, most people with 401(k)s haven't taken the time to think through their options. Most don't understand the fees they are paying. A fiduciary financial professional will spend time explaining the fees you are paying within your investments, and discuss with you the ramifications of that through a 20- to 30-year investment career.

## Saving When You Are Young

Millennials, the generation born between 1981 and 2004, are proving to be better savers than their Generation X parents. According to a March 2016 study by the personal financial website Bankrate.com, 62 percent of millennials are saving more than 5 percent of their income.

When I read that, I was encouraged to see that more than half of this generation is made up of savers, but a little disappointed in the amount they are saving. Five percent is better than nothing, but it needs to be at least 10 percent, if not 15 percent, and that is an average. According to the study, just a little over a quarter of those surveyed were saving more than 10 percent of their incomes, while

32 percent of people aged 30 to 49 were saving more than 10 percent.

Why do you suppose millennials are more savings conscious? Greg McBride, Bankrate.com's chief financial analyst, thinks it's because many of them grew up during the 2008 financial crisis and the ensuing Great Recession that lasted through 2010. While their parents came of age in the boom times of the 1990s, when home prices were escalating and the stock market knew only one direction, millennials saw how quickly a devastating financial storm can occur.

Is saving 15 percent of your income impossible? It may seem that way to many young people. No one ever said living below your means so you can salt money away would be easy. But I am encouraged to see things moving in the right direction for my 20- to 30-something friends.

I have noticed people who make more money usually tend to save more, but that is not always the case. It is more of a mindset. I also think millennials realize, "If it is to be, it's up to me." In other words, when it comes to retirement, this generation doesn't have the same expectation other generations have that they will be taken care of by the government or their employers.

## What Makes Each Generation Unique?

When the Pew Research Center did a survey of more than 2,000 adults in January 2010 and asked them, "What makes your generation unique?" the results were telling.[18]

It is true that each generation is characterized by its unique attitudes and experiences. What I thought was interesting was how each generation viewed itself and its commonalities.

[18] Pew Social Trends. February 2010. "Millenials: A portrait of generation next." http://www.pewsocialtrends.org/files/2010/10/millennials-confident-connected-open-to-change.pdf. Accessed Feb. 13, 2017.

Here's what the survey revealed:

The silent generation — 1925-1945

- World War II, The Great Depression (14%)
- Smarter (13%)
- Honesty (12%)
- Better work ethic (10%)
- Values/morals (10%)

Baby boomers — 1946-1964

- Better work ethic (17%)
- Respectful (14%)
- Values/morals (8%)
- The name "baby boomers" (6%)
- Smarter (8%)

Generation X — (1965-1984)

- Technology use (12%)
- Work ethic (11%)
- Conservative/traditional (7%)
- Smarter (6%)
- Respectful (5%)

Millennials — (1982-2004)

- Technology use (24%)
- Music/pop culture (11%)
- Liberal/tolerant (7%)
- Clothes (5%)

# Smart Ways to Retire

*There are plenty of ways to get to retirement, but not all of them are smart ways. Getting on the right path can be easier with these first three tips for retiring smart:*

**Smart Ways to Retire Tip No. 1:** *Create a retirement savings strategy. Consider how much you'll need to save by looking at what you want your income to be in retirement. Think about how much money you will need to have saved by the day you retire, and then think through what you may need to change in your current saving and spending patterns to get there.*

**Smart Ways to Retire Tip No. 2:** *Make retirement savings a top priority. Rearrange your budget to fit your new commitment to savings and stick to it. Consider eating out less, eliminating frivolous spending and finding other ways to bring in additional income through freelance work or odd jobs.*

**Smart Ways to Retire Tip No. 3:** *Create a general savings account and pay yourself first. Individuals with a healthy savings account are better equipped to cope with emergencies and can avoid dipping into savings earmarked for retirement. Set up an automatic deposit to your savings account each payday to happen before you make other payments or purchases until you have saved at least six months' worth of expenses.*

# CHAPTER TEN

# Who Is Your Worst Enemy?

"We have met the enemy, and he is US!"
~ Cartoonist Walt Kelly in Pogo

Have you ever met someone who is just negative? Negative about everything? You bring up an idea and they shoot it down before they even hear it? I believe people arrive where they are in life and become who they are based on how they treat other people, how they carry themselves, and their mental attitude toward opportunity. Interview someone you would consider to be successful, and you will find that there were intersections in their life where they made life-altering decisions. Stay or go. Spend or save. Give or keep for oneself.

Another hallmark characteristic of successful people seems to be accepting responsibility for what happens in their life. Instead of blaming others when things go awry with some plan, they realize that most things happen or don't happen based on choices we make. Instead of saying, "somebody's got it out for me," they say, "I could have done better. I will next time."

Self-discipline is another attribute of the financially successful individual. If you can't control yourself, how are you going to positively influence the flow of success in your life? This includes your health as well as your wealth. I realize we are 30,000 feet up here, and flying pretty high in the rarified air of philosophy-of-life talk, but I am sharing with you my personal experience. I think back to a time in my life when I was focused on the negative and lacked self-discipline. Conquering those demons, however, learning patience instead of anger, is the first step to replacing bad habits with good ones and entering the zone of successful behavior.

## No. 1 Pet Peeve

Here's a little brain-teaser for you.

Three frogs were sitting on a log. One of them decided to jump off. How many frogs were left? Answer: three. Why? Because the frog just **decided** to jump off. Doesn't mean it actually **did** jump off.

Procrastination can be our worst enemy if we allow it. Some people simply fail to take action once they arrive at the junction of education and opportunity. It's my No. 1 pet peeve because I have been there too. I have found myself in different seasons of my life postponing acting on what I knew to be the right path to take by waiting too long to move forward once the light has changed. Sometimes we wait for the perfect moment to move forward and we wait too long. The time is probably never going to be just right to do anything. We must make decisions based on the weight of the evidence, both pro and con. Think of a pair of scales — pros on the right, cons on the left. When the needle at the top of the scales points overwhelmingly to the pros side, then it is probably time to go ahead. Make a move. Take action.

> *"A wise person should have money in their head, but not in their heart."*
> *~ Jonathan Swift*

MONEY WON'T BUY HAPPINESS • 107

I don't know who said it first, but I have read it in several books, that there are three kinds of people: Those who make things happen, those who watch things happen and those who say, "What happened?" My observation is the most successful people in life are those who, instead of letting life happen to them, make life happen by taking decisive action at the right time. Please keep in mind I am not picking on anyone here, dear reader, but as Cinderella would say, "If the shoe fits ..." You can waste so much time and energy just not making up your mind — going back and forth and second-guessing every single inclination.

"But what if I make the wrong decision? What if this doesn't work out?" Most of the successful people I know have plenty of experiences to tell you of decisions they made that didn't work out perfectly. But they made educated decisions and didn't look back. If they found themselves at a dead end on one path, they simply changed directions and found the one that led to their goal. They are always on to the next thing.

## Cut the Check

One of my mentors once gave me the following great piece of advice: Determine what keeps you up nights, what it is that takes your time away from the more productive things you could be doing, and if that obstacle can be removed by cutting a check, then *cut the check!*

Essentially, he was saying turn over the responsibility to someone else — someone who is capable of handling it. That individual could be a staff member. It could be a third-party company. If you can afford to do it, relieve the pressure. You have bigger concerns with which to concern yourself; bigger decisions to make. Cut the check. Don't be indecisive. At the end of the day, I believe making a poor decision here and there is better than making no decisions whatsoever. It really is.

## Choosing a Life Partner

One of the biggest decisions we will ever make in life is choosing the person with whom we will spend the rest of our lives.

In medieval times, marriages were arranged, especially among the nobles. It was all about matching up kingdoms or land, or interlocking the fortunes of two families. Nowadays, it is part of the grand pursuit of happiness mandated by the Declaration of Independence, and typically has more to do with romance than money. That complicates matters a bit. What if you make the wrong decision?

One of the late Zig Ziglar's favorite stories is the one about the man who turns to his fellow passenger on an airplane and says, "Say, I can't help but notice you have your wedding ring on the wrong finger."

"Yeah, I married the wrong woman," the man replies.

I'm just going to say it. If you marry the wrong person, failure on many levels is soon to follow. And it's not that this "wrong" person is just a terrible person, it is just not the right fit for you. Your misery, your unhappiness, your feeling of being unfulfilled will eventually hamper your ambition and destroy your purpose. It will impede your progress toward your primary life goals. It goes without saying it will probably cost you quite a bit, dollar-wise.

So, how do you know you are choosing the right life partner?

"Wait a minute, Chris. I didn't know you were a marriage counselor."

Well, I'm not. I'm not a fireman, either. But, if pressed into service, I know how to put out a fire.

I can only tell you some things I have learned by what I have observed on the topic. One is, if you have doubts, you are probably right. Cold feet is nature's way of providing a fair warning — if you get a heavy feeling in the pit of your stomach when you imagine a future with a certain person, LISTEN TO IT!

The right person will make your life heaven and add value to everything you do. The wrong person can make your life a living hell.

## Have a Purpose

What keeps many individuals from achieving wealth and independence is failure to have a purpose in life.

We may feel as if we have a purpose if we have a job or a title on a business card. But that's not what I'm talking about. I am referring to a defined purpose — knowing why we are here on this earth, or what value we bring to

> *"Do you know what happens when you give a procrastinator a good idea?*
> *Nothing."*
> *~ Donald Gardner*

those with whom we interact. Some call it the big WHY. The central purpose we wake up to and walk toward every day is job one.

The bumper sticker I mentioned earlier, "Whoever dies with the most toys wins," got me thinking about the drivers. I wondered who they were, and what purpose they wake up to each day. If that is it — just the accumulation of stuff — then there is no way for those individuals to ever get where they are going. It will never be enough. And then you die.

Ambition for the right reasons can be a beautiful propulsion engine. Nobody — at least nobody in their right mind — wants mediocrity. Ambition allows those who possess it to push toward something, and when you think you are almost there, to push a little more until you are there. You push right into the end zone without looking back. You want to be the best you can be. You want to be the strongest you can be. Ambition will allow you to pay the price necessary for success. If you fail, it is ambition that makes you get back up and go at it again. Ambition allows you to persist in the endeavors attached to your big "WHY."

Don't get me wrong. I'm not saying work yourself to the grave or lose your family. It's all about balance, but ambition has got to be a driver here.

"Millennial" is the tag we have given to those who were born in the 20th century but arrived at their young adulthood around the year 2000. Most of them were raised with the idea that they were all set in life if they got a good education. To them, a college education was taken as a rite of passage — a birthright of sorts, but we are seeing that it takes much more than a college degree to be successful in life.

> "Empty pockets never held anyone back. Only empty heads and empty hearts can do that."
> ~ Norman Vincent Peale

According to data collected by Jason Abel and Richard Dietz of the Federal Reserve Bank of New York, in 2010, only 62 percent of U.S. college graduates had jobs that required college degrees, and only 27 percent had a job that was closely related to their major.[19]

The job market is extremely competitive. Academics have their place, but even more valuable is applying oneself wholeheartedly to what you are doing. Give me a person with ambition and passion any day of the week over someone with a degree who lacks those

[19] Brad Plumer. The Washington Post. May 20, 2013. "Only 27 percent of college grads have a job related to their major." http://www.washingtonpost.com/news/wonk/wp/2013/05/20/only-27-percent-of-college-grads-have-a-job-related-to-their-major. Accessed Feb. 13, 2017.

things. Make it a priority to constantly learn new things that will challenge you, and stretch yourself. That's how you are going to find success and navigate your way to independence.

CHAPTER ELEVEN

# What Is Your Exit Plan?

"It would be wonderful if we could avoid the common setbacks with timely exits."
~ Peter Lynch

You are still in your working years, around 10 to 15 years away from retirement. You have been working and saving now for 25 or 30 years and you have a nice little portfolio built up. The finish line is in sight. If retirement is the end zone, you are on the 20-yard line. Now is when you don't want to fumble the ball. You are more conservative in your play-calling because a turnover here can cost you the game.

Here is where making an emotional investment decision can wipe out years of effort and diligence. Here is also where it is essential to keep your eye on the dangers that could erode your wealth, such as hidden fees within your accounts or overpaying taxes.

If emotions weren't involved in investing, the smart thing to do would be to buy when the market is down, wouldn't you say? Isn't that the investing mantra? Buy low, sell high. The problem is, people are not formally trained in investing. They don't make the right decisions because it is counter-intuitive to do so.

## The Emotional Investing Cycle

EXHUBERANCE

EXCITEMENT

OPTIMISM

DENIAL

RELUCTANCE

FEAR

RELUCTANCE

INDIFFERENCE

DESPERATION

APATHY

PANIC

CAPITULATION

DEPRESSION

DESPONDENCY

**SOURCE:** BARCLAYS

The typical investor gets aboard the investment train when it is moving at a pretty good clip. Optimism keeps him or her aboard. As the stock rises in value, they feel good about their decision; what a clever investor they are! But the market moves in cycles. What goes around comes around and what goes up must come down. The stock falters and begins to lose value. At first there is denial. Then they might get a shaky feeling in the stomach as they see their account losing money. They panic and sell, feeling a need to leave the "sinking ship." Then, right about the time they are licking their wounds from cutting their losses, the stock begins to rise again. But "once-burned-twice-shy" mentality is hard to shake. They won't get back in until they see a definite pattern. Only problem with that is, once the definite pattern is established, with the stock on the upward run, it won't be long until the cycle comes back around, and the investor's cycle of emotions starts all over again.

That's why an index may be up 10 percent, but the general investing public will only have 3 or 4 percent to show for it. Emotions got in the way. Knee-jerk decision-making took over, and what happened was the complete opposite of what you wanted to happen.

## Balance Is the Key to Control

Retired investors can have more control of how much they will pay in taxes than at any other time in their lives *if* they structure their portfolios properly. The prudent retirees' portfolio will contain not just stocks and bonds; nor will it be dominated by just annuities, insurance products, commodities, or municipal bonds. It will contain a mixture of all of it. There will be some real estate in the mix as well. True diversification, in other words.

For instance, real estate complements a diversified portfolio. It is healthy to get a piece of the portfolio out of the stock market and put into something that is tangible. At the end of the day, when you own property — physical real estate — you are leveraging inflation. If that real estate is rented, then it is producing income year to year. That's great! It's like a dividend stock. The income is somewhat sheltered from taxes. Yes, of course you must pay taxes on the income, but you are also benefiting from depreciation on those properties.

A big problem I see with business owners is investing too much in their own businesses. I know some who have been successful in building a business from scratch only to see it prosper beyond their wildest dreams. They put *everything* into it, including all their profits. But the thing about businesses: they can fail. Most entrepreneurs, when we first sit down to talk, do not have traditional IRAs, Roth IRAs, 401(k)s or really any retirement-designated accounts. Their retirement plan is their business: once they are ready to retire, they'll sell this business that they've put everything into over the many years.

Selling the business and using the proceeds to bolster one's retirement income is all well and good. But what happens if your industry changes? What if you are forced to sell the business unexpectedly due to a health issue? What if new laws bring about unexpected regulations? As a business owner, you are so passionate about what you're doing that you put every penny into it. I can't fault you for your passion, but we need to find some true diversification here. There are plenty of retirement vehicles out there. Uncle Sam allows business owners to start SEP IRAs, for example, to take advantage of the same tax-deferred savings laws as employees of big corporations. Growing your business is great, but keep your retirement income source separate.

## Pick a Low-Cost 401(k)

I touched on this in Chapter Four of this book, but not all 401(k) plans are alike. They have become such a big deal in retirement exit planning these days, but it is so important that you choose a low-cost 401(k) plan. I'm talking more from a business owner's standpoint here, being one myself. You can select who is going to manage the plan for your employees. There is a big word that comes with that responsibility. It's *fiduciary.* If you are a business owner, you are the fiduciary for your people. Most 401(k) plans are extremely expensive. It is up to company management (you) to find a plan that will provide low-cost funds.

If you are an employee, you need to find funds within your plan with low expense ratios. Remember, every dollar you pay in fees is a dollar you are not saving for your retirement. As mentioned earlier, you won't find everything printed on your statement. Some have what is called a "brokerage link." That is, you are still working for your employer but you have an outside manager for your portfolio. It could be a retail manager or an institutional manager. This affords you many investment options you would not have otherwise, and could help you diversify your portfolio and, more importantly, lower the costs and fees associated with your 401(k) plan that may be taking a toll on the gains of your account.

# CHAPTER TWELVE

# How Important
# Are These Three Numbers?

"If your outgo exceeds your income, then your upkeep could be your downfall."

~ Anonymous

I didn't even think I would ever talk about credit scores, but I was having a conversation with a couple who are in their late 50s and are looking to refinance their home. They were asking me what kind of credit score they would need to qualify for the best interest rate possible.

Here's the thing. I'm a financial advisor, not a mortgage loan officer. I do have friends who are mortgage brokers, and I know enough about the subject to know that to get the optimum interest rate you need a score above 740, preferably into the 800s. I also know that is a damn good credit score and the people who have a score that high didn't get it overnight. They had to work hard for it. I also know that if I had a 59-year-old talking to me about it last week, there are probably some 20-, 30- and 40-year-olds out there wondering how they can get their credit score higher.

| Credit Score Ratings | |
|---|---|
| 760 to 850 | Excellent |
| 700 to 759 | Very Good |
| 723 | Median FICO Score |
| 660 to 699 | Good |
| 687 | Average FICO Score |
| 620 to 659 | Not Good |
| 580 to 619 | Poor |
| 500 to 579 | Very Poor |

People who have good credit scores in the 800s or high 700s do not carry balances over from one month to the next; they pay their credit cards off every month — in full. But an irony to building a good credit rating is that you need debt to do it. If you pay cash for everything, you never show up on the radar. But make it *good* debt. Responsible debt.

## What's Behind FICO?

The three numbers of your FICO score can make the difference between being able to purchase that lovely new home or continuing to live in the apartment you have been renting. These three little numbers can cost you or save you hundreds of dollars in interest, depending on how high or low they are. But what is FICO, and how are these scores determined?

What does FICO stand for? Well, nothing now. It used to stand for Fair Isaac Company, which was the name of the company that developed credit scores using data from the three major credit reporting agencies, TransUnion, Experian and Equifax. Now, however, it is like AARP and UPS. The acronym has become so well-known and commonly used that its original meaning has faded from use. In case you are wondering, Fair Isaac Company was founded by Bill Fair and Earl Isaac in 1956, and credit scores are only part of what they do. They also specialize in the science of predictive analytics and help corporations make decisions that affect their bottom lines.

Credit scores help lenders predict how likely it is that debtors will pay their bills on time.

Fully 30 percent of your FICO score is determined by the amount of money you owe. It's what they call the "credit utilization ratio." In layman's terms, it's the percentage of available credit you currently use. In general, your score is going to fall when you use more than 30 percent of your available credit. But don't look at that 30 percent as a target. Your target should be zero percent credit utilization.

How you pay a debt off is critically important to your credit score. First, you need to be responsible with those cards. There are two different types of cards out there — credit cards and charge cards. A charge card will make you pay the debt off every single month. With a charge card, the bill comes and the full amount is due. With a credit card, well you get a line of credit, and it can roll over. In fact, the issuers of the credit card *want* you to pay the minimum payment, and let the balance roll over. That allows them to tack on their 15+ percent interest rates on the debt, which can hammer you for years.

If it is your pattern to carry a balance on your credit cards from month to month, it may not be easy to start paying them off in full. But, from a financial management perspective, it essential that you get to that point. Let me just give you a few tips on getting to that point. By the way, I am speaking from experience here. I got my first credit card in the mail on my 18th birthday. I remember I had to pay some astronomical fee just to get it activated. It was the worst of the worst. After paying a hefty activation fee, I think I probably had a $300 limit on it. Then there was a processing fee. After the activation fee and the processing fee, I had paid around $240 in fees on a card with a $300 credit balance. True story. I was over 30 percent utilization the day I got the card in the mail! But that's another story. Here are the tips:

**Avoid adding more to the card.** What I mean is, if you are trying to get the credit card balance down to zero, you have to just **stop using the card!** The problem is, when we get the card paid down to a certain point, human nature urges us to use it again. We pull in to fill up the car with gas, and there goes the balance, back up again. Use the card to a point, and then make yourself pay cash for anything else over that limit.

**Cut back on your spending.** I know that's not a revolutionary idea, and it is easier to say than do. If you haven't evaluated your spending habits, this is an excellent time to do it. When that credit card statement comes at the end of the month, analyze how many of the transactions represent purchases you could have done without. Most credit card companies do a very good job of laying everything out. Some of them even categorize it for you: food, entertainment, medical, automobile, etc. Using that and your other receipts and bank statements, you can chart your spending patterns. Once you have it all in front of you, mark the areas where you can trim back your expenses.

**Use that cash to pay down your debt.** Track your progress. Commit to using the savings from a restructuring of your spending habits to hack away at your credit card debt. Can you see where you can cut back $100 here, $75 per month there, or whatever the amount might be? You will be amazed at how fast you can whittle down a mountain of debt with this belt-tightening technique.

**Increase your income.** If you are working at a place where you can adjust your hours, or take on more projects, consider working more until you relieve yourself of your debt burden. View the debt as the fire and the flow of money over it as the extinguishing agent. Work in a couple of extra hours of overtime. Is there a sideline job you could get into that could provide some extra income? Do you have a hobby that you could turn into a sideline job? Photography, for example? Or something administrative? Maybe you have an electrical background. Or perhaps you are a handyman. Sell something you don't need. Google "how to do a garage (or yard) sale." Let's go back to being a kid, and your parents were doing yard sales. We don't have to do yard sales these days. You know what a yard sale is called, it's called Craigslist and eBay, where you can sell things you no longer need. This is a great way to get an extra $200-$300 per month and sock it toward that debt. When I was in high school, I sold things on the internet and through classified ads. I'm not even that old, and I remember paying $10 for a classified ad and had people calling me on Saturday mornings until I sold everything I had advertised.

**Do the shuffle.** If you are carrying debt, you need to be doing the shuffle. I talk to many people who are carrying between $20,000 and $40,000 in debt and I ask them, "Hey, are you doing the credit shuffle?"

"What do you mean by that, Chris?" they will say.

If you are carrying a balance on one card, or multiple cards, consider consolidating them onto a card with a zero percent introductory balance. If you have gotten offers in the mail with a zero percent APR (annual percentage rate) introductory offer for the first eight or 12 months, it means the bank who sent you the offer wants your business. I have seen some extend the offer for up to 24 months. Do that. Why wouldn't you? Why hold a card that you are paying 21 percent interest on when you can move it to one that charges no interest? That buys you a 12-month or 18-month window you can use to pay down the debt with no interest. Guess what? Once you get to the end of that window, you do the shuffle again. You are going to save money on interest that you can apply to paying your balance off quicker.

**Spend only what you have.** This is No. 1: live at or below your means. Once you have paid off your credit card debt, make it a goal to never find yourself in that place again. Spend only what you can pay off at the end of the month. Create a budget. Establish your expectations and keep yourself accountable.

I have talked to people who have those high credit scores. Some of them have done the very things I am talking about here. Yes, it takes effort, but it is a huge piece of the puzzle that sets you up for financial success down the road.

CHAPTER THIRTEEN

# You Don't Know
# What Risks Lie Ahead

"But divide your investments among many places, for you do not
know what risks might lie ahead."
~ King Solomon, Ecclesiastes 11:2

What follows are a few thoughts on investing rules that
successful investors have followed for years.
The No. 1 rule of investing is *diversification.* I'm
not talking about just having a mixture of small cap, large cap, mid
cap and international stocks and some bonds. All those still put your
portfolio contingent on the stock market. I'm talking about true
diversification. A truly diversified portfolio will contain a mixture
of stocks and bonds, but also real estate, cash, commodities and
insurance vehicles. All of these in some way or another provide
different types of value and diverse rewards.

Some of the items I mention here protect against inflation.
Others can provide meaningful growth in good market years. Still
others will provide income.

A good fixed annuity or a fixed index annuity can be, and often
should be, part of the portfolio. I bought an annuity at a relatively

young age, and I have not regretted it. I also have a friend who, at a very young age, invested $300,000 in an annuity. How many 30-year-olds do you know with that kind of money? Probably not many. Why did he make that decision? Because by letting the annuity defer for 30 years, his contract will pay him $170,000 each year down the road for the rest of his life. That's not a bad deal!

> *"Money is multiplied in practical value depending on the number of Ws you control in your life: What you do, When you do it, Where you do it, and with Whom you do it."*
>
> *~ Timothy Ferriss*

Annuities are only a piece of the puzzle. All of the components of a truly diversified portfolio move at different speeds and in opposite directions. When one is going up, typically the other is going down. What is the value of that? It allows you to take risk without an emphasis on too much risk in any one category. You are able to maintain a balance in your investment picture, even when a bear market comes along.

**Rebalancing** is key. Shift your allocations year-to-year, whether it's your IRA, 401(k), SEP IRA, Roth IRA or others. Make sure the percentages you hold in each investment class are in line with your investment and personal goals, and harmonize with your objectives regarding growth and preservation. You may need to liquidate some positions to bring you within your risk tolerance as you age. If you are behind in your accumulation target, you may need to take on a little more risk. The important thing is to evaluate your portfolio each year and keep rebalancing your allocations.

**Dollar-cost averaging** is a simple and effective way to put your investing on autopilot. The key is to invest the same amount of money in the same investment on a regular basis.

Let's say you are contributing to your 401(k). With each paycheck, a pre-determined amount is contributed. The contribution buys shares of mutual funds. When the market is on an upswing, share prices escalate. Great! The balance of your account increases. When the market is in a downturn, your contribution goes farther and buys more shares. Great! Eventually, those shares will fatten when the market rebounds. The key is to continue steadily investing week after week, regardless of what the market does.

You can do that in a self-managed Roth or traditional IRA. You can do that in a self-managed nonqualified account. If you come into an inheritance, when you average the money into an investment through the years, you are dollar-cost averaging. This strategy forces you to put money into an investment even during hard times. You have time on your side. When the market recovers, you will reap the benefits of your discipline, consistency and persistence.

**Control the cost of your investments.** Right now, as you are reading this line, if I were sitting in the room with you and asked you how much your investments are costing you in the way of fees most of you would answer, "I really don't know."

Some of you might say, "Oh yeah. I'm paying 1 percent," but what about the fees within the mutual funds? What about the fees within other investments you are holding, the fees that don't appear on your statement?

Others would say, "Oh well, I'm paying a set amount each year. I have a fee-only advisor." If you do have a fee-only advisor, that's a great step in obtaining sound financial advice. But what about the investments your advisor recommended? What are the fees within those? Remember, every dollar you are paying in fees is a dollar that fails to come to you as a return on your investment.

The truth is, there are so many costs and fees associated with investments that most investors don't know what they are paying.

You may have been with your broker for years. You may have a personal relationship with your broker. I know some who play golf with their broker every weekend. They know the names of their broker's children, what kind of car they drive and what church they attend. But they don't know how much they are paying in costs and fees on the investments their broker has recommended.

*"Nothing in the world can take the place of Persistence. Talent will not; nothing is more common than unsuccessful men with talent. Genius will not; unrewarded genius is almost a proverb. Education will not; the world is full of educated derelicts. Persistence and determination alone are omnipotent. The slogan "'Press On' has solved and always will solve the problems of the human race."*
*~ President Calvin Coolidge*

I have a problem with that, and you should too. You may be best buddies with your broker, but you must hold him or her accountable for what your investments are costing you. How do you hold them accountable if you don't know what you're paying them? Another reason it is so crucial that you pay attention to these costs is they have a compound effect on your overall returns throughout the life of your investments.

Are there steps an investor can take to reduce or even eliminate some of these costs? Absolutely! For starters, you can save money on brokerage commissions just by using an online brokerage house. If you have enough money or you work with a Registered Investment Adviser, you may have access to an institutional manager or an institutional trading platform, which can drastically reduce your trading costs. If you are working with an institutional manager, you probably won't be paying retail.

If you are just interested in earning whatever the market's return is, buy an index fund. Index funds are mutual funds that simply track a market index, such as the S&P 500. For example, I often tell people who are inclined to be self-managers to buy a Vanguard fund. They charge low fees, often 0.1 percent per year. Self-management is not for everyone, however. If you are not yet retired and don't have time to think about your retirement accounts, you will probably prefer active management. Just keep an eye on those fees. Watch closely to make sure the trading in your account is productive and isn't just racking up commissions.

CHAPTER FOURTEEN

# How to Navigate the "B" Word

"A budget is telling your money where to go instead of wondering where it went."
~ Dave Ramsey

I know I have hammered a lot on the advantages of having a budget, but until now haven't gotten into the specifics of how to build one correctly and simply. Let me just share some techniques I have used personally and some suggestions that have worked well with families here in our office.

## Know Your Income

First, know your income. Before you can craft the structure that tracks and controls money going out, you must have a good grasp of the money coming in. I am talking about after-tax income here. Net income, not gross income. Now, this is easy is if you have a set salary, but it will be more difficult if your paycheck is variable. If the latter is the case, you must arrive at the income figure by adding up several months' income and putting together an average. *Do not figure in bonuses and tax refunds.* All of that is subject to change. Play it conservatively. Consider a refund or a bonus, if you get one, just

131

icing on the cake — that much more you can put away for you or your family down the road.

## Know Your Expenses

Secondly, track every dime you spend. Make a list of all the regular expenses. I'm talking water, utilities, rent, insurance, childcare if you have kids, groceries, car payments, the phone bill, internet. List everything. Maybe you're trying to pay down some credit card debt, or a student loan, or a home equity loan. Be sure to add those payments to the list. Total those expenses and make sure the money coming in is more than the money going out each month. You know what that means, don't you? If it isn't, you may have to eliminate some expenses that are unnecessary. You may have to sacrifice that double caramel macchiato you get at Starbucks every morning on the way to work. Or take a stay-at-home vacation this year instead of heading for a Sandals resort in the Caribbean. Whatever it takes to at least break even.

Now that we know our net monthly income and have an accurate picture of our expenses, we can navigate our way to a workable budget. This is where we make some value judgments on our spending habits. Remember, our goal is not merely to break even; our goal is to save for the future.

## Scaling Back

It would be marvelous if we were to total up our income and expenses and discover we are way under budget with plenty of cash left over, but that is not usually the case, is it? Usually, we have some belt-tightening to do. So where do we start? By listing our expenses into two categories: needs and wants.

Do we need that expensive cable package that gives us 25 movies to choose from plus every sports contest around the globe, or do just want it? How severe would the deprivation be to our family if we just went with basic cable?

Is eating out a major expense? How much of it is necessary? If the money going out is more than the money coming in, eat at home more. You may be surprised how much of your expenses are just like that. Money we spend without thinking of it, but money we could save with a little more conscious thought.

What about reducing the phone plans we have? We may be paying hundreds of dollars more for unlimited everything when we don't even use it. If you are looking for a way to save $300 or $400 a month, here are two words you need to know: "retention department." Call phone companies and cable companies that have retention departments that want to keep you as customers. Call them and tell them you have been shopping with other vendors and you have been offered a better deal. They will often scramble to sweeten your deal.

> *"The quickest way to double your money is to fold it in half and put it in your back pocket."*
>
> *~ Will Rogers*

"Oh, I'm so glad you called today, because we have a special going on this very month. We can cut your bill in half for the next 12 months."

The reason you didn't get a postcard in the mail advertising this special is because they don't tell you until they think they may lose your business. It may take an hour out of your afternoon, but if you do a little shopping with these services that we have come to consider necessities nowadays, you can save yourself some money. Remember, every dollar that slides out of the expense column slides over into the income column.

When you are building a budget, make sure you leave a place for contingencies. How old is your water heater? How many miles do you have on that second car? How soon will you need new tires? Is your air conditioning system more than 10 years old? Estimate a reasonable amount for those types of expenses that tend to sneak up on you.

This is where you should have an emergency fund set aside just in case the roof needs replacing or your car breaks down. I recommend at least six months (preferably nine months) of your salary set aside in a liquid account, like a checking or savings account. A credit card is not an emergency fund. Expect the unexpected. This applies whether you are in your 20s buying your first house or in your 50s looking at retirement.

*"Money is a guarantee that we may have what we want in the future. Though we need nothing at the moment, it ensures the possibility of satisfying a new desire when it arises."*

*~ Aristotle*

We just redid the kitchen floor and, wouldn't you know it, the refrigerator went out. It's always going to be something if you are a homeowner, and you don't want those little things to derail your budget.

## Controlling Impulses

My mother-in-law is one of the most frugal people I know. She wouldn't mind me telling you that. In fact, she takes pride in it. She pays attention to the thermostat and understands the relationship between that little dial on the wall and the electric bill at the end of the month, if you know what I mean. She is not an impulse buyer. She compares prices before she buys. She would never be the type to be swayed by her emotions into buying a new car. Not her. First, it would have to be a transportation need before she would even consider it. Then, she would carefully research the purchase and evaluate which make and model represented the most value for her dollar, or bang for the buck as she would put it, "You can either have the money, or you can have what it will buy — but you can't have both." According to her, thinking about an expenditure before you make it is the best way to save money.

## Tracking Your Dollars

It has never been so easy to track your dollars. You don't have to have a big old book on your desk — a ledger — in which you laboriously enter and add every figure. You have computer programs these days that will do it all for you with a few simple keystrokes.

I remember my grandfather. He had terrible handwriting, but he would spend hours hunched over a big green book, noting every log entry in his jittery script. Nowadays, you have Quicken, Mint and numerous other budget apps. These electronic tools allow you to synchronize the data with your checking accounts and credit cards and categorize every expenditure. The totals appear automatically at the bottom of the spreadsheets.

With these types of programs, you can pay your bills with electronic checking. Your checkbook is instantly balanced and the expense categorized. You do not have to crunch numbers on your own. Take advantage of these things. There may be a little bit of a learning curve getting into it, but they provide a great advantage to those wishing to grab hold of their spending once and for all.

# CHAPTER FIFTEEN

# Shave $300 Per Month Off Your Budget in 30 Minutes

"Don't tell me where your priorities are. Show me where you spend your money, and I'll tell you what they are."
~ James W. Frick

Earlier in this book we were discussing how to reduce your cable and cellphone bills by contacting the provider's retention departments and negotiating. It made me think about some other things that perhaps people don't realize are negotiable from year to year. Credit card interest rates, for example, and fees within your credit cards are not set in stone. You get a statement once a year that typically says what your APR for the coming year will be. It could be anywhere from 14-24 percent. You probably file the statement away, or toss it in the trash, and pay it. After all, we don't question the electric bill or the water bill. Why would we presume to question what the credit card company wants to charge for their services?

No harm, no foul if we don't carry a balance. But if you do carry a balance, paying that kind of interest, especially if you pay the minimum payments, can be a killer.

"Okay, Chris, so what should I do?"

Call them.

Just call them, and let them know that you are trying to get ahead with your payments. Ask them to reduce your interest rate for a small period. Most of them will. I'm telling you, all you have to do is call them. Ask, do they have any zero interest balance transfer offers? I have seen credit card companies cut APR in half many times for customers who just ask.

Just asking could save you hundreds, if not thousands, of dollars. But here's the deal — when you make that call, you need to have a track record. They will evaluate who you are based on how promptly you pay. It helps if they view you as a great customer, and be nice. Don't be demanding. They are used to people calling them up and complaining, perhaps because they were charged a late fee. Customers who raise their voices and use harsh language usually get nowhere.

If you are having trouble making your payments with the current rate, use that as leverage. They would rather you pay than default. Use expressions like: "I am trying to do everything I can to stay current, and bringing the interest rate down for me would really help, even if it is for six months."

If you do not meet with success on your initial try, tell whoever is on the other end of the line you appreciate their trying to help. Say sincerely: "I appreciate the fact that you have done everything you can to help me. Thank you very much. Could I please speak with your supervisor for just a moment?"

When the supervisor comes on the line, go back to the beginning with your explanations. Be clear on what you want and why you want it. State your case with just as much earnestness as you did before. If you *still* do not meet with success, tell the supervisor the same thing you told the previous customer service agent. You appreciate that they did all they could to help you. Ask to speak to the supervisor's supervisor. Keep running up the food chain until you get someone to say yes. Be patient and be nice. Never lose your temper or raise your voice. It works most of the time.

It never hurts to ask.

## Annual Fees

Annual fees on some of these cards are anywhere from $65 up to $500 per year. A lot of these cards charge big annual fees because they come with a lot of perks. I have a couple of cards that have high annual fees because I travel a lot for business and my family does a lot of personal travel.

I use those perks that come with the cards, so they are of value to me. But I will still call the company once a year and say, "Hey, could you give me a $200 credit on this card?" You would be shocked at how often they say yes.

"Sure, you are a great card holder and a loyal customer."

They know they will get my business next year if they comply. I know they will never cancel me if the payments are coming in and I pay their annual fee. At other times, I have just asked if they can waive their annual fee. Guess what? They do it 50 percent of the time! It helps if you have been a good customer for many years.

## Lowering the Rent

I know some of you out there don't own a house. You are paying rent. How long will you stay there? Two years? Three, maybe? If so, paying rent is not such a bad idea. But if you are going to be at a location for four, five or six years or more, you should consider buying a property. That will be easier or harder depending on the market and location of the property. I realize that owning the property requires commitment, but as you save throughout your working career, you will also be climbing the economic ladder, too.

Hopefully, you will be earning a higher salary. Also, don't forget the mortgage is a tax deduction for you.

*"Beware of little expenses. A small leak will sink a great ship."*
*~ Benjamin Franklin*

If you are paying rent, is it possible to negotiate the amount you pay? It is more possible than I think many people believe. This is especially true when it comes to apartment complexes. If you live at a large complex, there could be between $50 and $200 of wiggle room in your monthly rent. If you are in a complex with lots of units, that's more bargaining power for you.

When you are touring an apartment, always tell the manager, or whoever is showing you the showcase units fully furnished, that you have looked at a couple of other places that are just as nice, just as convenient and fit your budget. That is your first bargaining chip — competition.

Maybe you have talked to a couple of the other units who say they will come down $100 a month just to earn your business. Hey, that's $100 a month times 12 — $1,200 a year possibly saved right there just for asking. Doesn't hurt to ask, okay?

Another bargaining chip for renters is offering to prepay a few months in advance. That can be huge. I was a landlord for years. I had several renters. If someone came in and said they would be willing to prepay a year, or six months, I would cut a few hundred dollars off the rent without hesitation and be willing to cut more if asked.

It could be the owner is trying to lease for six months to a year. If you say, "Hey, look at my credit. It's great! My financials are great! I'll rent it for 24 months." Do you think they would be willing to negotiate a better lease?

You may be willing to keep up the maintenance on the property, such as mowing the yard, keeping the paint fresh, fertilizing the lawn, those kinds of things. Is the cost of those services built into the rent? If you could handle a couple of those things, could you get the rent lowered by $200 per month? Maybe $100? Let's say it saves you $150 per month. Multiply $150 per month times 12 and you have $1,800 in your pocket at the end of the year.

## Clipping Coupons

I'm not a big coupon clipper. My mother-in-law is. I do most of my shopping online these days, but this is a big one. If I am buying from an online merchant, the first thing I do is type in the merchant's name into Google's search for a coupon code for the item. You are going to see dozens of websites pop up offering coupon codes. Merchants offer deals to attract your business. The coupon codes don't work all the time, but many times they do, and the savings are usually 15-20 percent off. That can add up quickly if you are an online shopper.

If you are getting ready to buy from an online retailer, go to a wholesaler and see if you can get a better deal. Try Overstock.com or eBay. Many new online merchants these days offer the same products because they don't have a brick and mortar store; they simply have a distribution deal with the manufacturer. Depending on what you are buying, one online merchant may sell the same item for hundreds of dollars less than another online merchant. With large purchases, before you hit "submit order" button, try to find the exact same item for less or with free shipping.

If you are at Best Buy, you are at a big box retailer. Look for damaged goods (sometimes they say that but aren't) and open the boxed items. Nine times out of ten, those items will be excellent condition, but just have a little tape around the outside of the box because it has been opened before. Depending on what you are buying, you can save $50 to $100 right there.

## Medical Bills

Medical costs are through the roof, and everyone who gets one of those bills in the mail probably thought it was going to be covered by their insurance provider, only to find out that only a portion of it was covered. Or, it was negotiated down and the deductible wasn't met. Did you know that you can call that medical provider and negotiate the bill?

These companies are used to dealing with the best negotiators on the planet — your insurance company. They won't be shocked when you call to negotiate your bill.

You have an unexpected medical emergency. You go to the emergency room. Before you know it, you are getting a bill for $6,000 or $10,000. Those bills can be drastically reduced by negotiating as long as you approach the creditor with an attitude of appreciation. Thank them for their willingness to work with you. Be honest as to what you can really afford to pay them.

Benjamin Franklin said, "A penny saved is a penny earned." Negotiating will require work and patience. But the dollars you save can be saved and invested and contribute to the security of your financial future.

# CHAPTER SIXTEEN

# Money in Your Marriage

"They say that love is more important than money, but have you ever tried to pay your bills with a hug?"

~ Anonymous

I f you are married, and have been for any length of time, you know that marriage can be the No. 1 hiccup when it comes to finances. When married couples argue, money is usually at the top of the list of what the argument is about. "All healthy marriages have disagreements over money," says Laurie Puhn, a New York City-based couples mediator and author of *"Fight Less, Love More."*[20]

Money is the No. 1 conversation that many people try to avoid in a relationship. It's just not fun to discuss who spent too much money at the department store on a clearance sale, or whether the latest gadget was a necessary expense. It's always a conversation that goes nowhere.

---

[20] Geoff Williams. US News & World Report. June 17, 2014. "Why Couples Fight About Money." http://money.usnews.com/money/personal-finance/articles/2014/06/17/why-couples-fight-about-money. Accessed Feb. 13, 2017.

## The Clueless Spouse

I cannot tell you how many pre-retirees come to my office without their spouses to discuss their financial picture. You might think the one who shows up at the office alone is the one who handles the money in the family, but you would be wrong. Nine times out of 10, those who show up for the appointment alone are the partners who trusted their mates to handle the finances. Now they are closer to retirement, don't have a clue about where they are financially, and are seeking answers. Fortunately, most couples come in together. That is how it should be. But situations where one partner handles the money and the other partner doesn't even know where the checkbook is are very common.

*"A big part of financial freedom is having your heart and mind free from worry about the what-ifs of life."*

*~ Suze Orman*

God forbid if the one who handles the finances gets hit by a bus. What would the clueless spouse do? Where is the money? What is the name of the account? What is the log-in? Where is the password? How much is in the account?

That's why it is so much better if there is communication with you and your partner about these matters. This communication can have a positive ripple effect, not only for you personally, but for your children and other family members.

None of us are immortal. As Hank Williams sang, "I'll never get out of this world alive." At some point, we will not be around to make the decisions and steer the financial ship. It would be prudent to bring those closest to us up to date on such matters while we are present and able to do so. It is just the responsible thing to do.

## Plan Together Before Marriage

For those of you who are not married, the sooner you can start these financial conversations with your future spouse, the better. I speak from experience here. I knew my wife for many years before we married. If you can come up with a game plan together about how you will allocate your funds for things like savings, paying off debt and goals you both wish to achieve, it will make for a smoother marriage.

There is certainly nothing wrong with setting "his and hers" goals. Another way to eliminate confusion and future trouble is to open two separate accounts — one for fun and leisure, and the other for necessities. Try to fund these accounts each month according to your mutually agreed upon goals. Of course, the necessities account will be the priority, but you may be surprised at how beneficial to the relationship the fun account will be. You need to take time for fun in your relationship. Having an account for such purposes will eliminate those awkward and angry conversations about money and contribute to the success of the relationship.

## It's How You Recover

I see a lot of couples. When we sit down at the conference table, I usually tell them what the purpose of our meeting is, and what we will try to accomplish in our first and second visits together. One of the expressions I hear most often is, "We have made many mistakes." The "mistakes" to which they are referring usually have to do with handling money. They may have put money in an investment that went belly up, or they may have lived beyond their means and not saved enough for retirement. One couple said they were invested too heavily in the stock market in 2008 when the bottom fell out. They got completely out of the market, and now the market's back and then some — a recovery they have missed out on.

Such mistakes are common. And, yes, they can keep you from making progress, financially. But here's what I tell people: I have the unique privilege of seeing hundreds of portfolios every year, and everyone — and I do mean everyone — has, at some point in their lives, experienced financial setbacks. The key to being successful in managing your finances is how you *recover* from these setbacks. What steps are you going to take from this point forward to prevent them from happening again. My mantra is "learn from your mistakes and move forward."

For many of you, reading this book constitutes a first step in getting professional help in putting a plan together. Whether you have $10,000 or $5 million in the bank, recognizing that you need professional help is a first step to financial success.

You may be an engineer, a physician, a plumber, an electrician or some other specialist. That is your area of expertise. I don't know the first thing about running electrical lines in a house. That's why I would hire an electrician if I needed that done. I have lots of plumbing in my house. I have a toolbox somewhere, and I'm sure that I could find a wrench inside it, but that doesn't mean I would pull the wrench out and say, "Well, I'm going to go for it here. I'm going to try and fix it myself so I can save a buck." Chances are, I would "fix" the problem into a more costly repair than it originally was. I am a big believer in seeking professional help where necessary.

No one I know of would try self-dentistry. They would not be so careless with their health. But there are some who are careless with their wealth and think financial self-management is the way to go. Your life's savings is what will hopefully secure a successful retirement future for you. Take that first step. Hire a professional.

CHAPTER SEVENTEEN

# Ahead of the Game and Don't Even Know It

"Time is a currency you can only spend once, so be careful how
you spend it."

~ Harmon Okinyo

I realize I have spoken frankly in this book. I can't apologize for
that. If you went to see a doctor about your health, you would
want him or her to shoot straight with you, wouldn't you? If
you feel that way about your health, you probably feel the same way
about your money.

Abraham Lincoln was one who loved tact, but, at the same time,
did not tap dance around the truth. A quip often attributed to the
16th president was: "If you call a tail a leg, how many legs does a dog
have? The answer is four. Calling the tail a leg doesn't make it one."

So far in this book, in the interest of shooting straight, I have
pointed out many things that I feel folks do wrong with their
finances. Now we're going to have a little change of pace. I would
like to propagate some hope for those who I feel are doing things
right. There are a lot of you out there who are in that category —
doing things right — and you might not even know it. Handling

one's finances can be overwhelming. It is easy to think you aren't doing it right, or you may think you need a finance degree or a background in managing money to get it right. There are a lot of you out there who are doing much better at managing your money than you know. I have seen some of you here in my office. In fact, one of the best things I get to do from time to time is pat someone on the back and tell them that they have done a phenomenal job and their accomplishments have brought them to this point.

You are on track and okay. You may need some fine tuning, but you are doing things most investors out there haven't even begun to do. I'm talking about things such as saving money, paying off credit card debt immediately, never carrying a balance, and communicating with your spouse about money matters. Planning together. Educating yourself. Constantly reading and trying to get better. Learning new ways to manage and invest your money. Lowering your bills every month, or at least looking for ways to do so. Knowing how much you spend.

> "One of the funny things about the stock market is that every time one person buys, another sells, and both think they are astute."
>
> ~ William Feather

That last one, knowing your spending, is a big one. If you can just tell someone how much you spend at the end of the month, you have a huge jumpstart on financial success.

As you are reading this, even if you have plenty of money coming in through a healthy salary from a good job, it all comes back to your budget. Why? Because it's not how much you make that counts; it's how much you get to *keep* of what you make.

No matter how old you are, you have at least had the thought of what retirement would look like someday, haven't you? Can you picture yourself there? Not having to report to the office or go to work? That also means no more paycheck. If you know what you will have coming in at that point, you are well ahead of the game. Many Americans don't have a clue. If you do, I commend you heartily. Have you had that conversation with your spouse? I remember telling my wife one time how excited I was about retirement.

"But you are at least two decades away from retirement," she replied.

"I know, but I am still excited about the prospects of it all," I said.

And I meant it. Although I truly enjoy my work, I am counting down to that day. How about you? Have you planned ahead for that eventuality? If you have, then you are doing it right. That planning is, in and of itself, a huge accomplishment.

# About the Author

As a financial advisor, Chris works with families and individuals retiring today, as well as those retiring 10 to 30 years from now. He believes, whether you are 25 or 65, it is never too late (or too early) to begin planning and, most importantly, saving for retirement. As a fiduciary advisor, Chris prides himself on an unwavering commitment to integrity, stability, long-term relationships and the highest standards of service and performance.

In addition to his work with clients, Chris co-hosts the "Retire Ready" radio show on News Radio KLBJ 99.7FM & 590AM. This format allows callers to get the answers to their retirement questions LIVE on air, at 2 p.m. every Saturday and 3 p.m. Sundays.

As a contributor on KXAN News Channel 36, viewers can tune into "Retire Ready TV," at 8:56 a.m. Saturday mornings. Every weekend, Chris discusses innovative ways to position yourself to retire ready and successfully in today's economic environment.

Chris is a contributing columnist for Kiplinger personal finance magazine, and has appeared in Fortune, Money Magazine and Bloomberg's Businessweek.

Chris is a member of the Better Business Bureau and the Financial Planning Association.

At the end of the day, saving for retirement is only half the battle. Withdrawing in retirement presents an entirely different set of challenges. Families and individuals look to Chris for expert guidance and to help keep them on a path toward financial security and independence. Chris and the team of advisors at REAP Financial strive to provide organization, accountability, objectivity, proactivity, education and partnership throughout retirement.

Chris Heerlein lives in Austin with his wife, Hannah, and three children. Chris is an active supporter of numerous charitable endeavors and is an accomplished musician.

Made in the USA
Columbia, SC
24 August 2018